Up to Speed with Mirth Connect (and NextGen Connect)

by

Mitch Trachtenberg

ISBN 9798686289260

Print version 1a, Oct. 2020. Based on Mirth Connect version 3.9.1.

Table of Contents

Introduction..v

Setting up...1

Creating a first channel...9

Extracting data from messages; transforming messages..15

Reading and Writing Files...33

Switching to a Production Ready Database..40

An HL7v2 channel..45

HL7v2: a very brief introduction..58

Filtering Results..63

Code Templates...73

Alerts and Responses..79

Building an HL7 message from Database Data..93

Epilogue...99

Appendices...101

Introduction

Mirth Connect is open source software that can accept, change, and forward information packets, called messages. Such packets might consist of anything from spreadsheet data, to medical messages, to emails. It is frequently used to send messages in a format called HL7, and it has some built-in understanding of HL7 messages to simplify work with such messages.

Written in Java, Mirth runs on any system capable of running a Java virtual machine, including Microsoft Windows, Apple's OS X, and Linux.

We're going to take a step-by-step approach, tackling some of Mirth's fundamentals before looking at how it handles HL7 messages. Even if you're an old hand at HL7, there are aspects of how Mirth dices and slices messages that can create boobytraps. The more you've seen Mirth under the hood, the less likely it is you'll fall into traps.

This book is not a reference tome, and I make no attempt to cover Mirth's capabilities in a comprehensive way. It is aimed at someone who knows the basics of programming, has been confronted by Mirth, and is trying to make sense of it. It won't make you an expert, but it may prevent you from wanting to kick your computer. Mirth is a large tool with a lot of areas; I'm hoping that this book will let you familiarize yourself with a few central things, without intimidating you. The goal is to get you ready to learn more on your own.

We assume you have downloaded Mirth and the Mirth user guide from https://www.mirthcorp.com or https://www.nextgen.com. If you haven't done that yet, please do. Both downloads are free. Think of the User Guide as a reference, and use this as a tutorial. Because this is tutorial in nature, you'll get the most out of it if you work it from the beginning, rather than try to jump in someplace in the middle. Some topics which you might expect would have their own chapters are covered, instead, when they first become useful in the context of the tutorial.

A note about names: Mirth Connect has been renamed to NextGen Connect by NextGen Healthcare, which is the current name of a corporation which acquired Mirth Corporation. They are the same product, and Mirth is protected by an Open Source license, so you will always be free to download and use the core Mirth Connect software. NextGen and Mirth are registered trademarks of NextGen Healthcare, Inc.

A note about screenshots: Because the Mirth user interface uses a small font, our screenshots use a modified version to make them more readable. See the appendix for information about how we did this.

A note about names: for purposes of this book, we'll refer to the product as Mirth Connect or just Mirth.

I'll be grateful for any comments or corrections; please email mjtrac+mirth@gmail.com. Errors will be noted at my web site, http://mitchtrachtenberg.com.

Setting up

This guide assumes you have downloaded and installed Mirth (and Java, if it hadn't been on your system), started Mirth as a service on your system, and have an "m" m icon displayed in your toolbar. If the "m" is orange, the Mirth server is running; if it is gray, click the icon and then click "Start Mirth" in the popup that appears.

Once it is running, Mirth is a server process that listens for incoming messages and processes them according to rules you provide. Your interaction with a running Mirth server will usually be via a different program called the "Administrator." With the Administrator, you can create and deploy various channels through which information will flow. There is also a program called the "server manager," which is displayed in your toolbar, and which offers you the option of starting, stopping, or restarting the Mirth Server.

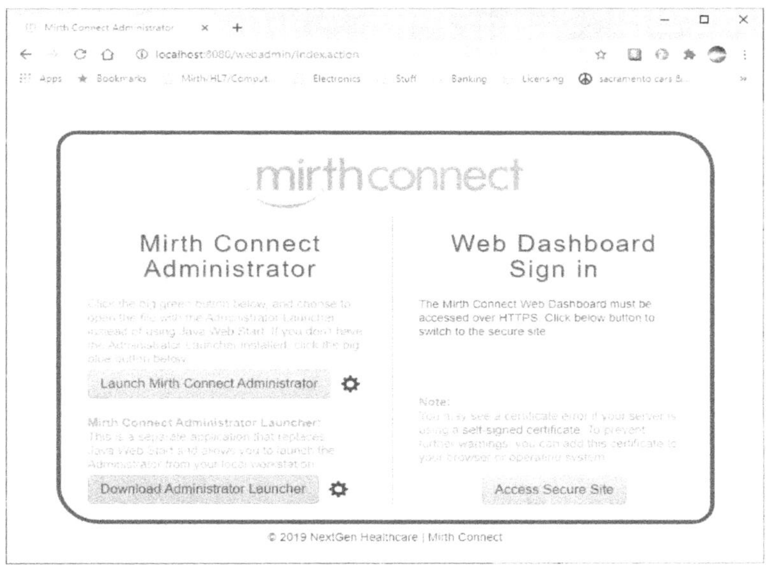

Logging in to the Administrator

You may start the Administrator on the server's host from the "Server Manager." If you don't have access to the server manager, you can launch the Administrator or download a special "Administrator Launcher" program from the website Mirth establishes at the server's port 8080. For example, if you are on a machine "alice" and a Mirth server is running on a machine bob, you can open a web browser on alice and type http://bob:8080 to bring up a web page that will let you open an Administrator on alice to control the server on bob. (This also works if you are on the server machine, just type http://localhost:8080 into your browser.)

The exact procedure, unfortunately, will vary based on the version of Mirth you've downloaded. Older versions use a "webstart.jnlp" file, but due to changes in Java, 3.9.1 and later will use the Administrator Launcher approach.

The "administrator launcher" default install looks like this (if you are using Mirth's defaults, the ports will be 8080 and 8443):

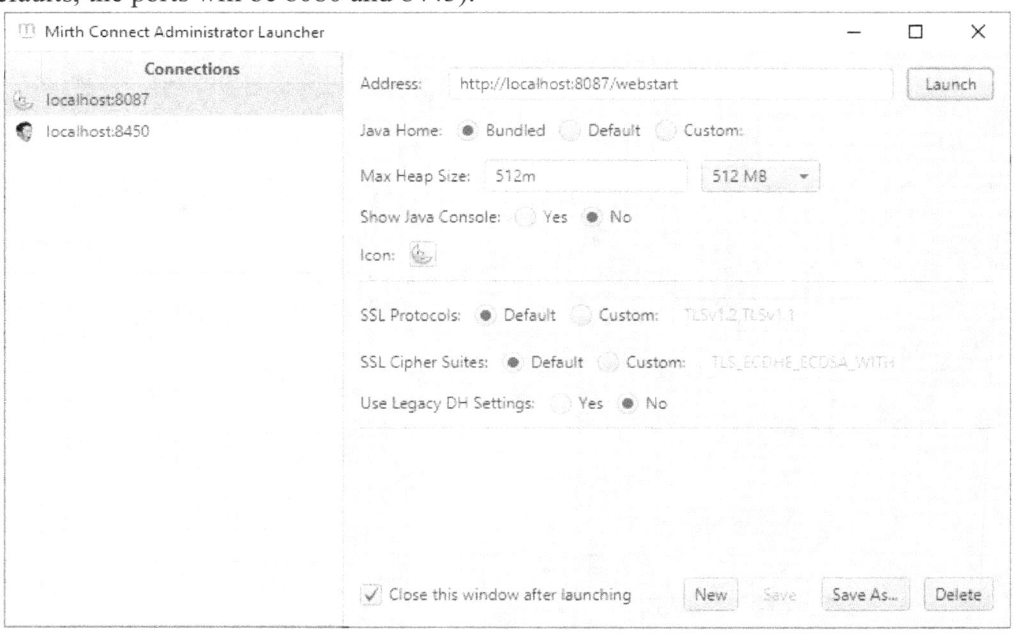

Click on the Launch button to bring up a login window. You will be asked to log in; the default username and password are both admin.

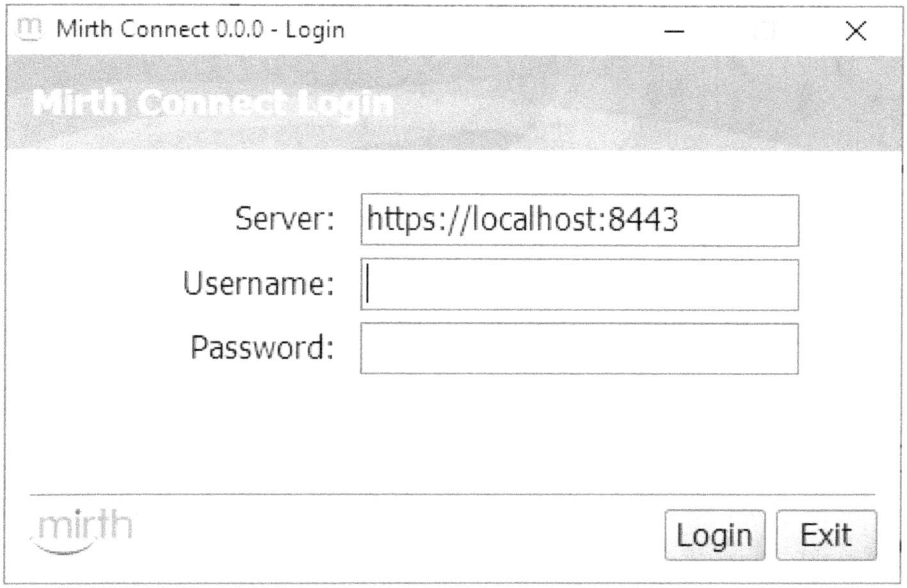

Whichever way it was started, when you log into the Administrator for the first time it will solicit information -- the only fields you actually need to fill in are the user, password, and password confirmation fields.

Dashboard and Channel Views

We'll start now in the Administrator. In the upper left, you have your choice of seven screens, Dashboard, Channels, Users, Settings, Alerts, Events, and Extensions. We'll do most of our work switching back and forth between the Dashboard and Channels screens.

The Dashboard screen shows you how many messages your "deployed" channels are processing, and what state they are in. The Channels screen lets you edit or create channels. You can get to the messages quickly from either screen using a popup menu and selecting "View messages."

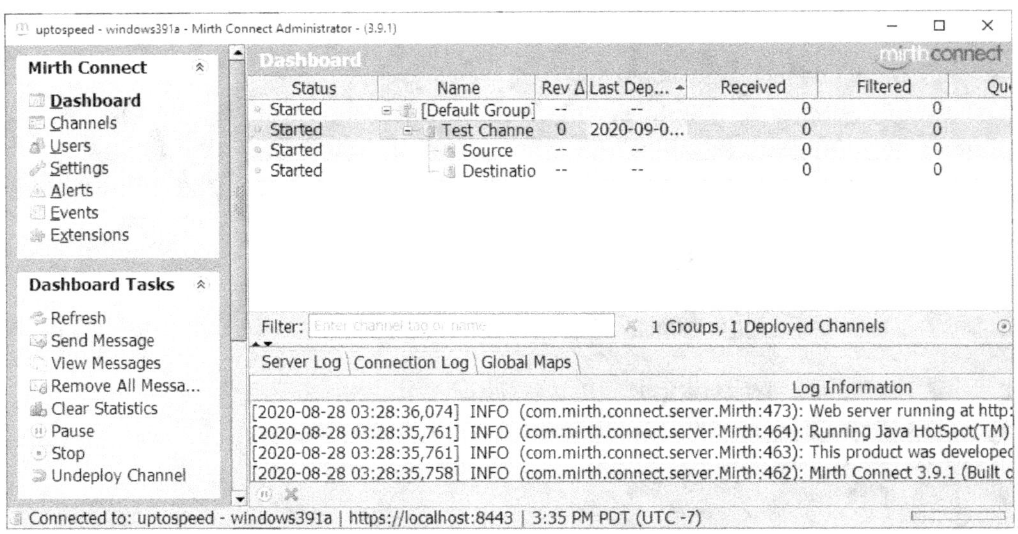

Using the option in the "Mirth Connect" box at the upper-left of your window, you can switch between the "Dashboard" and other views. The initial screens will look largely empty when you have not created any channels. But notice that underneath the "Mirth Connect" menu, there is a tasks menu which changes to tasks appropriate to the view you've selected. Until a channel exists, these tasks will not appear.

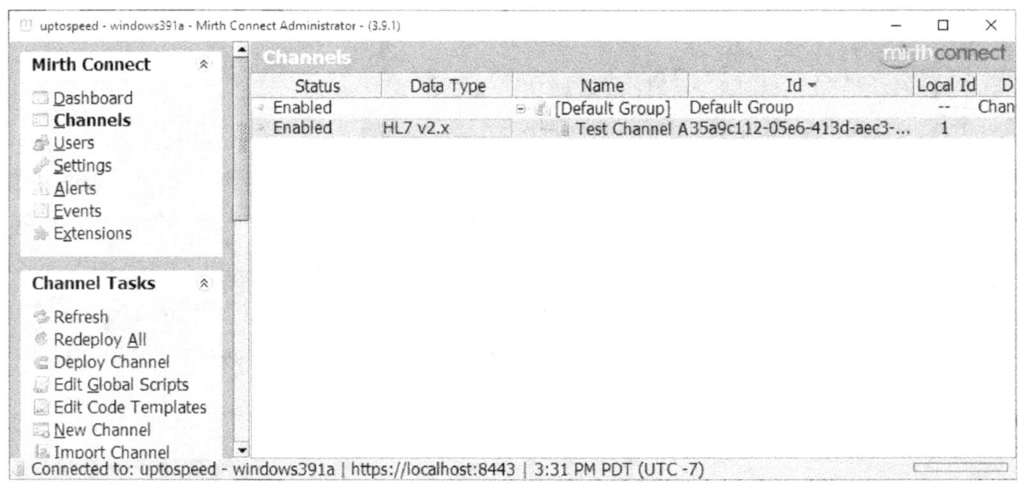

The Dashboard lets you see what channels you have deployed in service, their current status, and how many messages each has received and sent. The Dashboard is "message oriented." When it is displayed, the left area of the Administrator will have a sub-area called "Dashboard Tasks," through which you can send a message to a channel, view a channel's messages, and stop a channel or remove it from service entirely.

The Channels screen lets you see all channels you've created, whether they are deployed in service or not. When you click on "Channels" in the upper left "Mirth Connect" subarea of the Administrator, you'll notice that the "Dashboard Tasks" subarea is replaced with the "Channel Tasks" subarea, offering you the ability to create and edit channels. You can also deploy them (place them in service), disable them (so that they cannot be deployed), and export them to an XML file that can be imported into another Mirth instance.

Both the channel and dashboard views can be narrowed by making use of "Channel Groups" that allow you to focus on one type of channel. For a new Mirth, we have only the "Default Group;" should you create more than a dozen channels, you will probably find it useful to group them.

Besides Dashboard and Channels, there are other screens which play less critical roles. We will introduce them when we find they are needed. If you wish for Mirth to be able to send email, though, you'll need to go to the Settings screen and enter information about an SMTP server you'd like Mirth to connect with.

Sending a Test Email

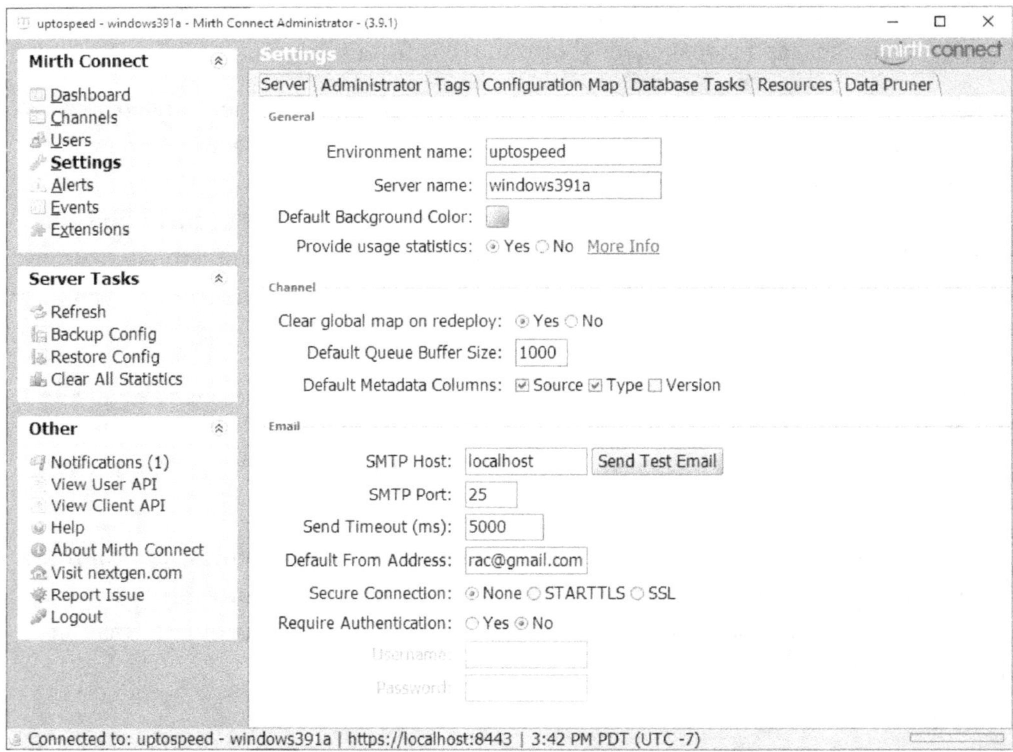

The easiest way to test that Mirth on Windows can send email, if you don't have access to a mail server, is to download the free program Papercut, by ChangeMaker Studios, from https://papercut-smtp.com. Run the program. If a firewall dialog appears, and asks about allowing it to communicate, allow it access.

To confirm that Mirth was able to send mail into Papercut, I configured email settings in the Server tab of Mirth's Settings screen, clicked "Send Test Email," entered my address mjtrac@gmail.com as the destination address, and the following email promptly arrived in Papercut's window.

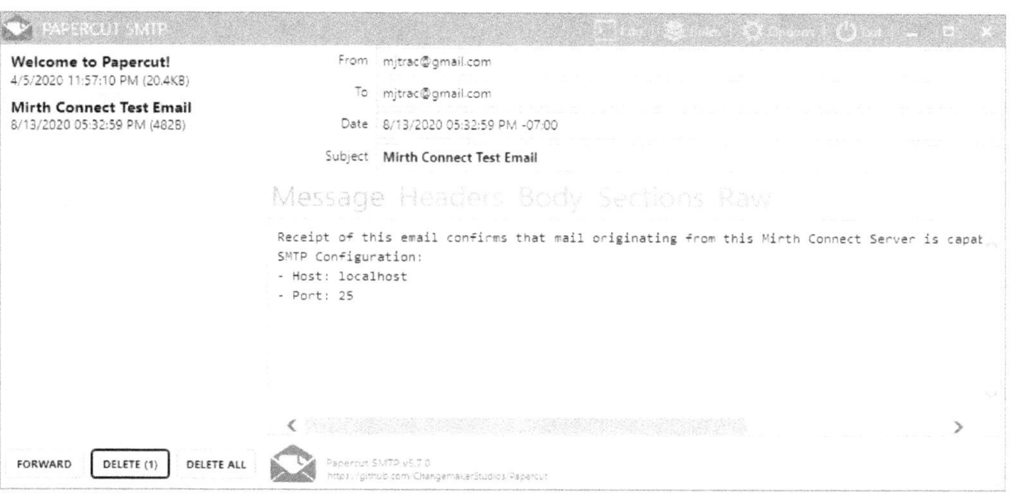

Of course, if you actually want to have mail sent beyond your computer, you'll need to set Mirth up with a connection to an active SMTP mail server; one that will then forward mail beyond your computer. This could be a local SMTP mail server you install on your machine, or a remote SMTP server you connect to over the internet.

For example, to establish a connection to the Gmail SMTP server, you will first need to ensure that your Gmail account is configured to accept connections from "less secure clients."

Then, in your Mirth Server Settings screen, set the SMTP host as smtp.gmail.com, the SMTP port to 465, Secure Connection to STARTTLS, and enter your gmail username (your full gmail email address) and your gmail password. Note that if Gmail tightens its security requirements further, this may not work in the future.

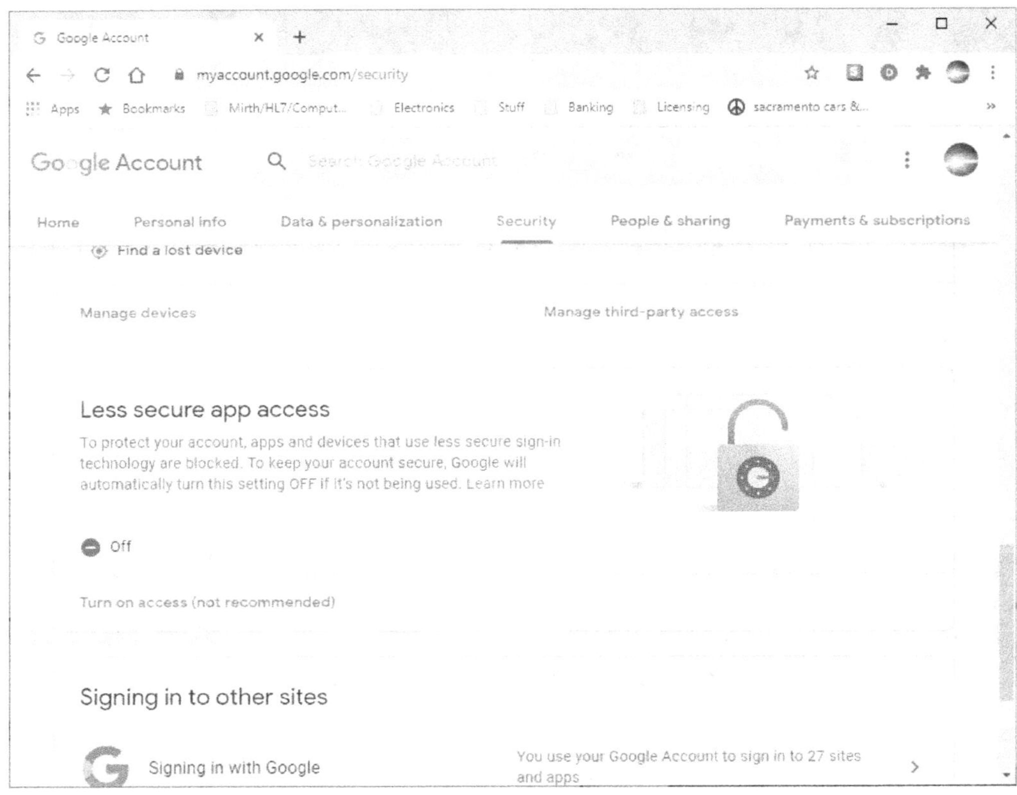

Another task that might be considered setup is connecting Mirth to a database like Postgresql, Mysql, or SQL Server, rather than using the default provided in the distribution. You will want to do this, but we will deal with it in a later chapter.

So, that's it as far as a first pass at the Administrator's user interface. This is a topic that is covered extensively in the Mirth User Guide, so if you'd like to learn more, head on over there.

But if you're itching to create your first Mirth channel, read on.

Creating a first channel

We will begin at the very beginning, creating a channel to copy some text from any files that land in a folder, adding it to an "accumulator" file in another channel. This is a simple enough task that we'll be able to learn how to work with channels without having to pay much attention to anything else, especially the intricacies of HL7. This is a different approach than many might take -- I urge you not to skip past these sections, because jumping right into HL7 handling can leave you in a surprised state when your operations don't behave as you'd reasonably expect them to.

> Please note: we will change some default values to work with "raw data;" that's because Mirth as shipped generally expects you'll be working with HL7. We'll get to HL7 soon enough; for now, raw it is.

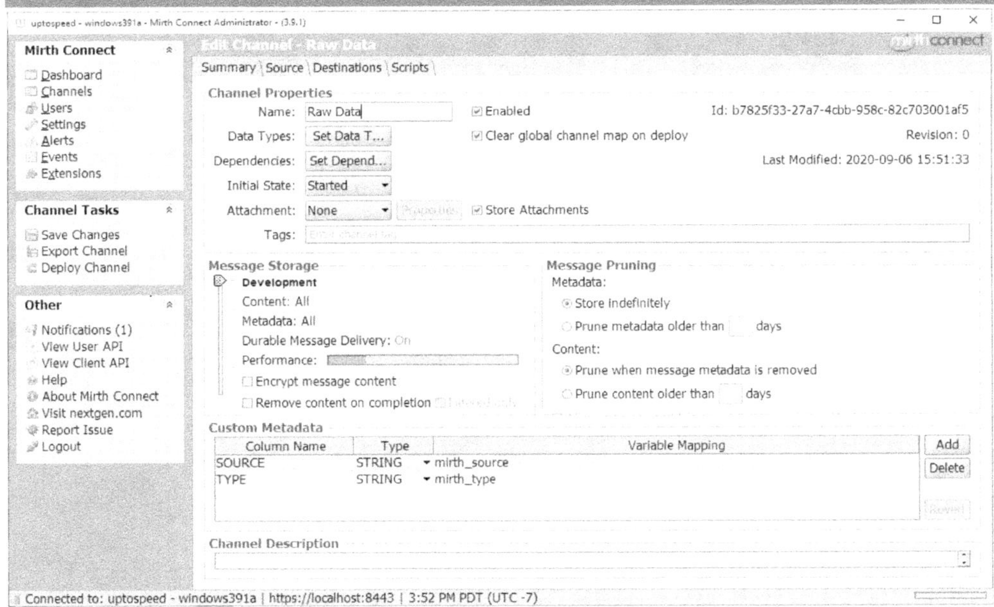

Switch the Administrator to the Channels view, and click on "New Channel" in the Channel Tasks subarea. You'll arrive in a tabbed view that has Summary, Source, Destination, and Scripts tabs, with the Summary tab selected.

Let's give our channel the name "Raw Data," after which we can click on the Data Types button under the name field. The first thing we see is a table listing the connectors of our channel. Every channel has a source connector and at least one destination connector. For our new channel's connectors, the data types are all set to the default: HL7 v2.x. Let's change them all to Raw, by choosing that from each of the four dropdowns offered, and then click OK. Different data types require some amount of further configuration, but Raw is Raw, and has no further settings.

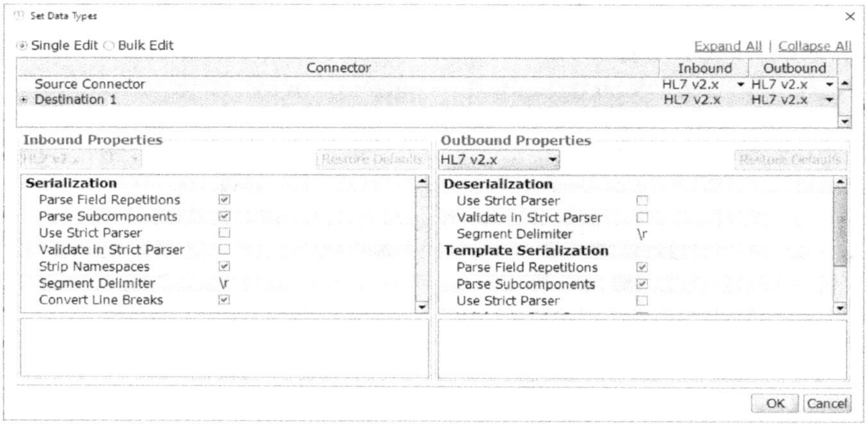

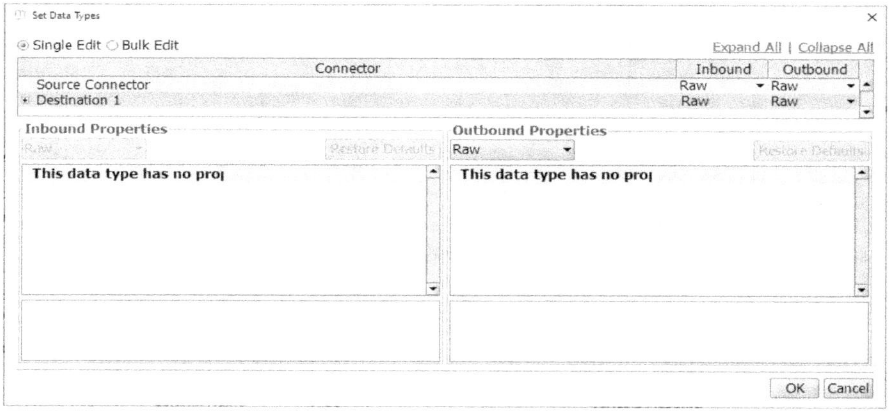

Before going to the next tab, let's look at the Message Storage and Message Pruning areas of the Summary tab of our new channel.

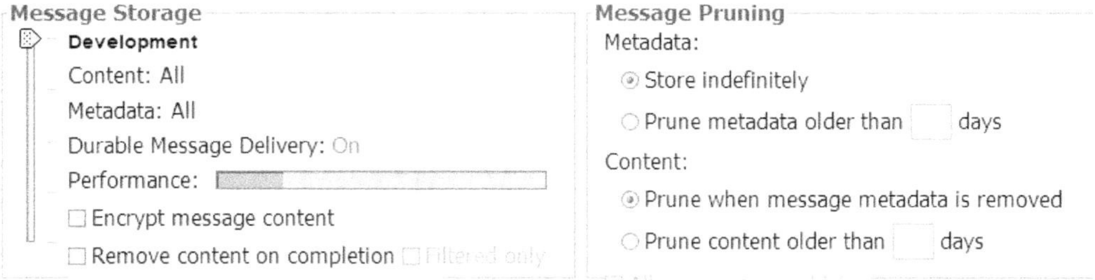

Message Storage
Development
Content: All
Metadata: All
Durable Message Delivery: On
Performance:
Encrypt message content
Remove content on completion Filtered only

Message Pruning
Metadata:
Store indefinitely
Prune metadata older than days
Content:
Prune when message metadata is removed
Prune content older than days

The Message Storage box has a slider on the left which is set to "Development" and shows "Durable Message Delivery" is on. Performance is indicated with a qualitative slider; "Development" mode's performance is not the best. That's because many, many different versions of the message are stored in Development mode. Put a little dog-ear in the book at this page, because when you begin noticing databases getting to wild sizes very rapidly, you'll want to come back here. Suffice it to say that, particularly as you process HL7 messages as opposed to raw data, you may be shocked by how much space Mirth demands in order to store all these versions of every message. You'll almost certainly want to move to a setting lower on that vertical slider once you've debugged your channel.

Now, moving to the right of Message Storage, we find Message Pruning, which starts at "store indefinitely." In any real production environment, it is likely that you will want to prune and archive messages rather than leave them in the channels eternally. If you are sending medical data, there may be storage requirements, so make sure you understand them before you prune without archiving.

The last thing to notice on the summary screen, for now, is the channel description. This is an opportunity to document the channel for others, and the start of your description will show in the Channel view. Let's write "A sample channel to see how Mirth handles raw data."

Great. Let's save our changes by clicking "Save Changes" in the Channel Tasks area to the left, and then let's deploy the channel into service by clicking "Deploy Channel" in Channel Tasks, and confirming by clicking "Yes" when the confirmation screen appears.

When we deploy a channel, we are taken to the dashboard view. The time of deployment will be highlighted for a few minutes, to help us spot newly deployed channels. Prior to taking the next screenshot, I clicked the boxed plus sign to the left of our new channel name, so that the display has expanded to show the channel's connectors.

Dashboard

Status	Name	Rev Δ	Last Dep...	Received	Filtered	Queued	Sent	Errc
Started	[Default Group]	--	--	0	0	0	0	
Started	Raw Data	0	2020-09-0...	0	0	0	0	
Started	Source	--	--	0	0	0	0	
Started	Destinatio	--	--	0	0	0	0	

Let's send a message. In the dashboard window, click on your new channel's name, "Raw." The channel will be selected and Send Message will appear in the Dashboard Tasks subarea.

Click "Send Message." In the Message window that pops up, type "Hello, Mirth" and then click "Process Message." Notice that you can read your message in from a file, and that you can control which of the channel's destination should receive the message; by default, it will be sent to all destinations. You can also set variables for the source map; for now, you can think of this as part of the environment in which your messages are processed.

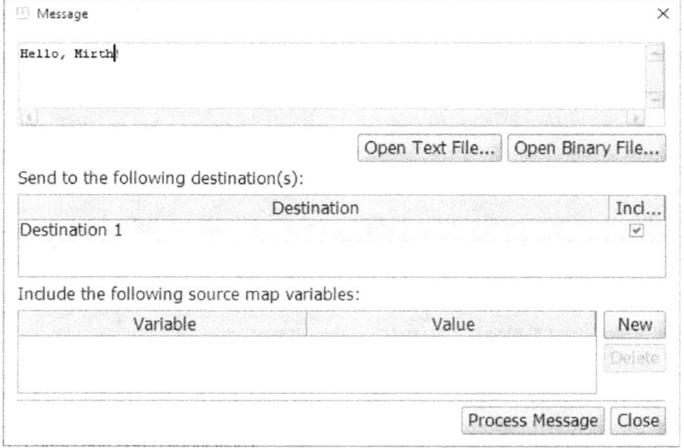

For several seconds, nothing evident will happen. When the Dashboard refreshes, though, you'll see that 1 message was received and 1 message was sent. (You can manually refresh the dashboard if you are impatient -- click "Refresh" in Dashboard Tasks -- and you can use the Administrator tab of the Settings screen to control the frequency of automatic refresh.) If we click the boxed plus symbol to the left of the channel name, this information is broken down by connector: the source connector received 1 message and sent it along to the connector for destination 1, which sent it to whatever destination it has been set to send to (nowhere, for the moment).

Status	Name	Rev Δ	Last Deplo...	Received	Filtered	Queued	Sent	Errored	Connection
Started	[Default Group]	--	--	1	0	0	1	0	--
Started	Raw Data	0	2020-09-0...	1	0	0	1	0	Idle
Started	Source	--	--	1	0	0	0	0	Idle
Started	Destinatio	--	--	1	0	0	1	0	Idle

Make sure "Raw Data" is highlighted, and click "View Messages" in Dashboard Tasks. This gives us a new view, "Channel Messages," for our Raw Data channel. There are search criteria that enable us to narrow down our view to particular messages, but there's only one message at the moment, id #1. Click on "Source" to see how it looked at the source connector. The message appears in the bottom half of the window.

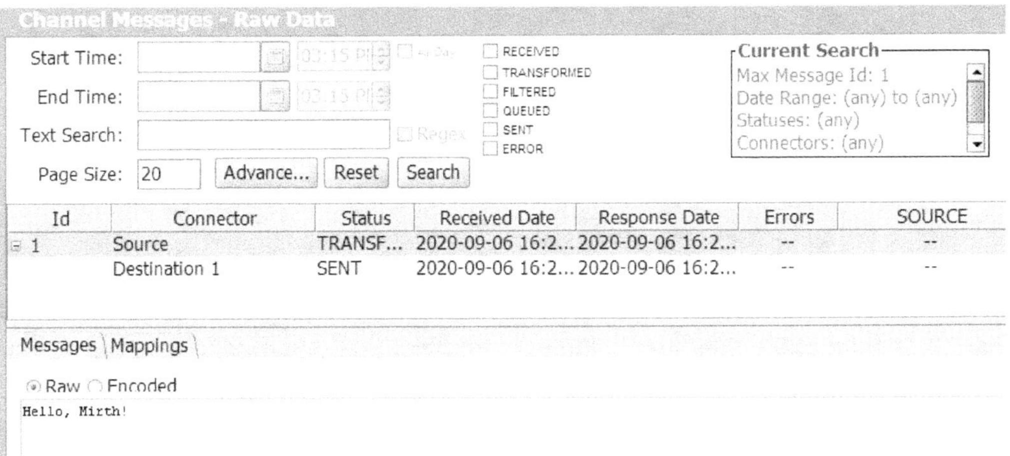

Our first message, seen "Raw," is "Hello, Mirth!" Encoded, it is also "Hello, Mirth!" Because we have set our channel's data type to "Raw," there is no encoding. Click on the Destination, Destination 1, and you'll see that the message is unchanged at the destination connector, raw or encoded. You'll also see additional radio buttons, allowing to see different things related to the message. "Sent" allows us to see exactly what was sent to where, and "Response" allows us to see what we were returned by the system we sent the message to. We won't always get response messages but, in general, when working with HL7, every send will be accompanied by an HL7 acknowledgement message, indicating success or failure and possibly providing additional information from the receiving system.

We'll return to some of these things, but for now, let's go to the Channels view and export our channel. Then, we can click on the Channel Tasks "View Messages" task and in the Message Tasks menu in the resulting view, we can select "Export Results" to export our message. The exported channel and message are in the appendix. There's no need to examine them at this point, but you may find it interesting to examine the XML which Mirth has created in exporting. Much of the Mirth user interface's configuration is hidden behind layers of choices, but the configuration becomes evident in the exported channel XML. There's quite a bit of information.

Extracting data from messages; transforming messages

Our next step will be to work with some spreadsheet comma-separated-value data. This will enable us to observe and get used to the way in which Mirth encodes structured data. In some situations, Mirth users will want to generate HL7 messages from CSV, spreadsheet, input. But even assuming we never use CSV format data again, this is an important intermediate step towards understanding how Mirth works with HL7 and other complex data, please do not skip over this material.

Return to the Channels screen and create a new channel named Delimited.

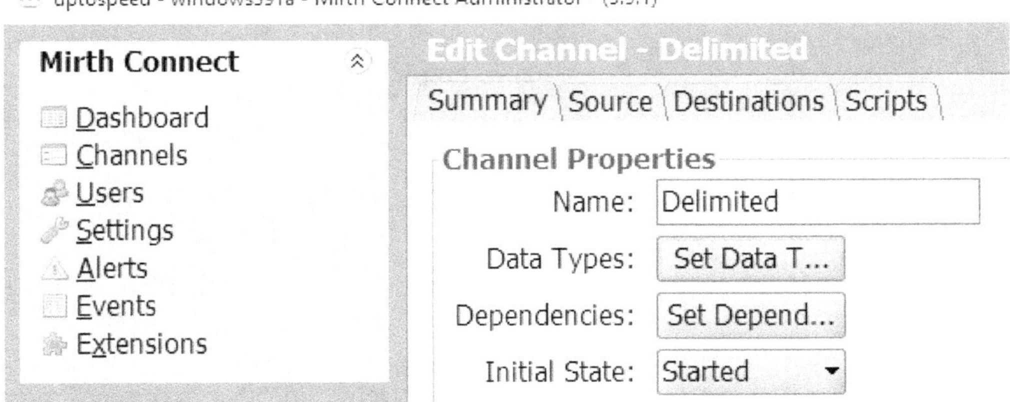

On the channel summary screen, click on the button immediately below the name entry text field: "Set Data Types." By default, Mirth sets channels to work with HL7 data. Let's change our Delimited channel so that it works internally with data in Delimited Text form. In the "Set Data Types" popup window, the source and destination connector inbound and outbound sides are each set to HL7. Change each of them by dropping their choice menus and selecting "Delimited Text." When you do, you will see that there are many options for specifying, among other things, how the text is delimited. We'll stay with the defaults, with columns delimited by commas and records delimited by newlines.

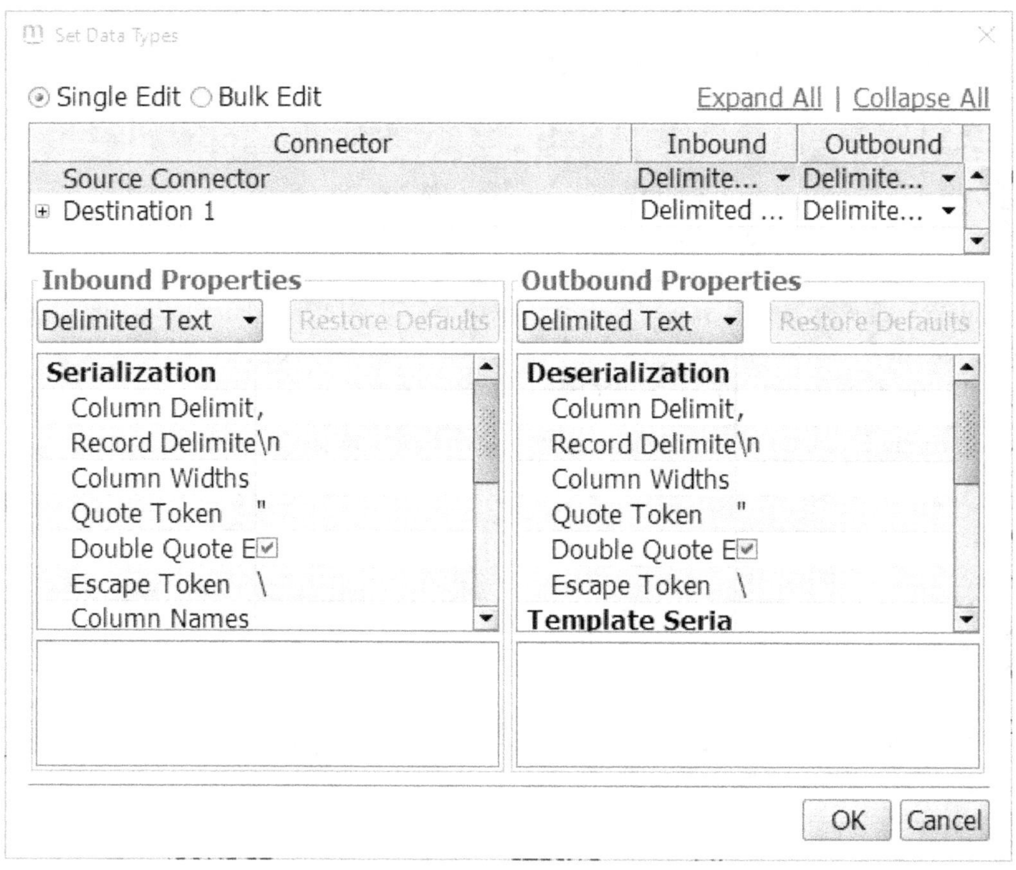

Answer "OK" once you've set all four dropdowns to "Delimited," then save your channel (Channel Tasks/Save Changes).

Unfortunately, we're going to have to trick Mirth into thinking we're actually doing some processing with the message; unfortunately that means a bit of unexplained magic. I promise we'll make sense of "Transformers" and "Filters" very soon, but for now, please just follow this set of instructions:

You should still have your new, Delimited channel open for editing. (If not, then in the Channels view, highlight Delimited and select the Edit Channel task.) Click on the Source tab. Click on "Edit Transformer;" then, under Transformer Tasks, click on the Add New Step task. On the right, double-click on the word "Mapper" and select "Javascript" from the dropdown. Then, add a comment line in the "Step" window.

Javascript comments can begin with two slashes "//" and are purely to document what is happening in the code; in this case, that would be absolutely nothing. Under "Mirth Connect Views" click Back to Channel. You can also double-click in the "Name" area to enter a name for your step. Repeat this process on the Destination tab. In both cases, the dummy transformer step will look like this:

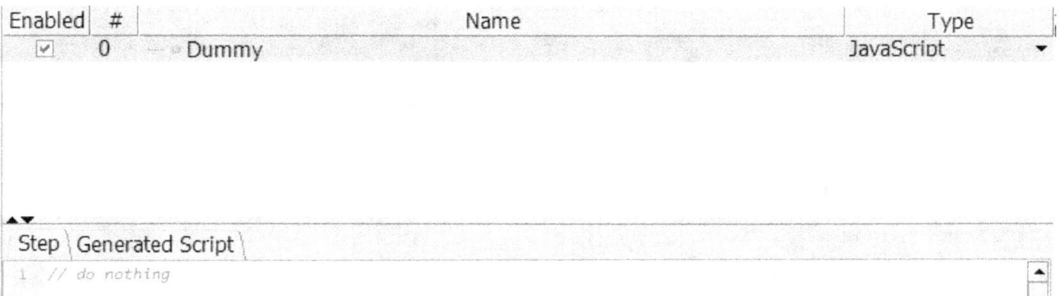

What we've just done is force Mirth to handle our message as it will handle most real-world messages it processes, although no actual transformation is being done, Mirth has no way to know that. Our comment-only Javascript doesn't actually affect anything message-related. But now, we can track how Mirth processes messages through the channel.

Save the channel (Channel Tasks/Save Channel) and deploy it (Channel Tasks/Deploy Channel).

Select your new channel on the Dashboard, and send it a message using the "Send Message" area of the Dashboard Tasks. We can re-use the phrase "Hello, Mirth!" since that conveniently has a comma. After sending the message, highlight the channel and select "View messages" from the Dashboard tasks. Highlight the first message's Source entry.

First highlight the "Source" side of the message, and see what displays at the bottom when you click the Raw and Encoded radio buttons. Then highlight the destination side and click through the larger set of radio buttons: Raw, Transformed, Encoded, Sent, and Response.

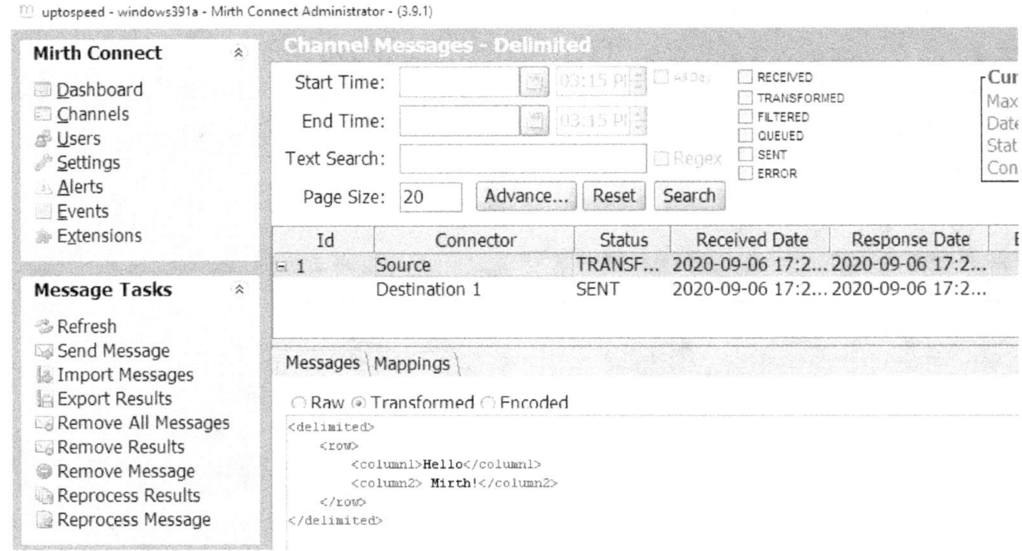

Mirth has taken the data from the CSV message and converted it -- serialized it -- to XML, in order to assist in further processing:

```
<delimited>
    <row>
        <column1>Hello</column1>
        <column2> Mirth!</column2>
    </row>
</delimited>
```

The message is rooted at “delimited,” which has one child node “row,” because our test message had only one row. That child node has been split at the comma into two fields, “Hello” and “Mirth!” (actually “ Mirth!” with a leading space, since the comma is stripped but not the leading space). Had we had two “spreadsheet rows,” each would be in a `<row></row>` block.

Mirth also converts HL7 messages to XML for processing.

We’ll now take a look at how to manipulate or observe the structured contents of the message. We do this using, in Mirth terminology, a “transformer.” Before starting a real transformer, though, let's note that channels don't ordinarily get messages because you've manually sent one via "Send Message." Channels get messages based on the connector type of their source connector.

From the channel screen, click on your Delimited channel to highlight it. You've been editing channels by selecting from the Channel Tasks; you can click Edit Channel there or right-click the channel and select Edit Channel from the pop up menu.

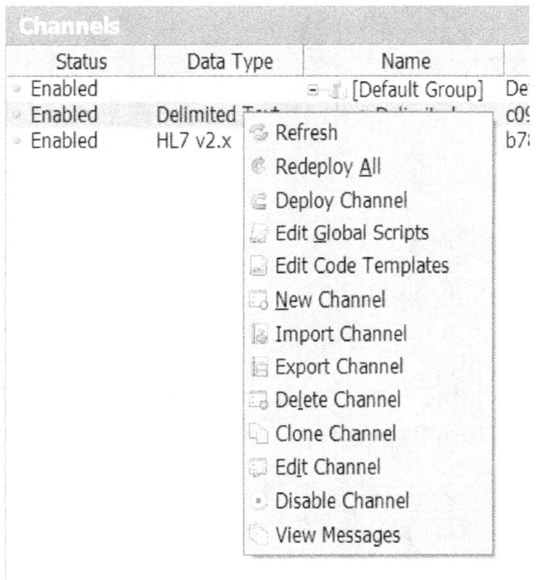

By default, our channel's source connector type is "Channel Reader," this means that the channel expects to be sent messages from other channels. Click on "Channel Reader" to see a list of other available channel types; we'll just notice for now that there are many different ways for a Mirth channel to listen for data. Among other ways, you can read from files or file-like sources, listen for incoming TCP/IP or HTTP, and so on.

Different connectors will anticipate different types of structured information, and so will convert incoming data to different XML trees.

Let's get access to the XML by creating a real transformer. To the left of the channel's pane, the Channel Tasks area has "Edit Transformer." If you've been following along until now, you've already created one transformer, so the tasks area will actually show "Edit Transformer (1)." Click this task and, if you did create the dummy transformer step earlier, highlight it and select Transformer Tasks/Delete Step to get rid of it. We'll replace it with a Javascript step.

Select Transformer Tasks/Add New Step. This time, go to the "Type" field, drop down the dropdown which has the default value of "Mapper," and choose Javascript instead:

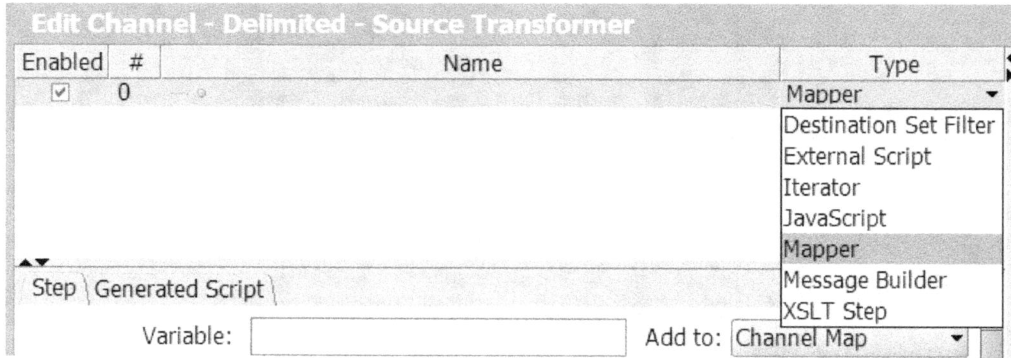

We're going to look at two ways to have Mirth present a sliced-and-diced message. We'll do it manually first, then use the Mirth user interface to simplify things.

Writing a Javascript Transformer

Our incoming message's XML tree can be accessed in Javascript as the variable named "msg." This variable is pointing at the topmost level of the tree, "delimited." To access the value of the leaf node named column1, and store it in a variable, we write the following into our Javascript window:

```
var col1 = msg['row']['column1'].toString();
```

If you are new to Javascript, the English translation is, roughly, create a variable named col1 and store into it what you find when you take our message as it has been transformed into XML, travel to the row block, travel to the row block's column1 node, extract its value and convert it to a string, that is, to text.

We now need to take the content's of the col1 variable and make it available not just in our source transformer, but to our destination connector and its various transformers. We do this by setting it into a dictionary shared by the connectors, called our channelMap.

We write:

```
channelMap.put('first_column', col1);
```

This creates an entry named "first_column" in our dictionary which is named channelMap, and sets the entry's value to the value of our variable col1.

A slightly abbreviated way to say the same thing is as follows:

```
$c('first_column', col1);
```

To confirm you've got all your t's crossed and i's dotted, click on Transformer Tasks/Validate Step. If you do not get a popup saying "Validation Successful," you have probably mistyped something. As we'll see in a moment, the Mirth user interface makes it possible to "write" this Javascript without having to learn this syntax, but I believe understanding what Mirth is doing will be critical, which is why I'm asking you to do it this way first.

Let's give a name to this transformer, by double-clicking in the highlighted row of the "Name" column above our code and entering "Save column1 to channelMap."

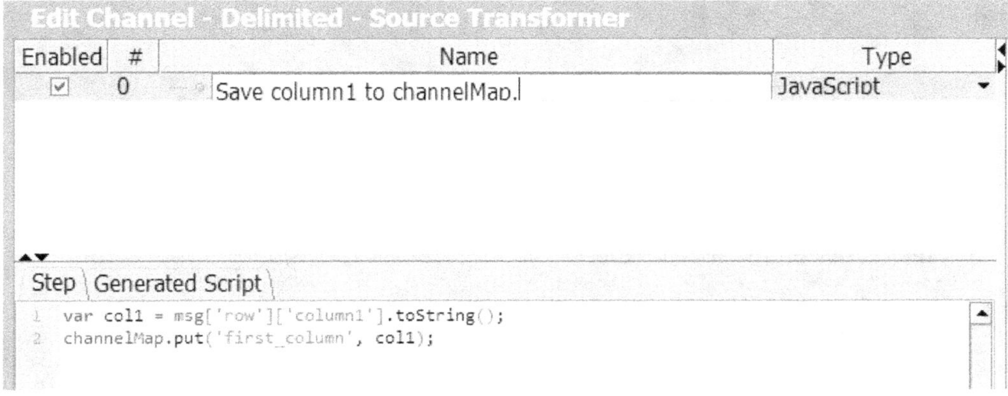

We can now return to our channel and select the Destinations tab. The first and only destination is "Destination 1" and is of type "Channel Writer." As with our source connector, we can choose a variety of destination types; for now, we'll stay with Channel Writer, which passes the message along to another local channel of our choice.

At the bottom of our screen is an area named Template, with the following text within:

```
${message.encodedData}
```

By default, the channel writer will replace this with the encoded data of our message. Let's change our template so that we write instead the value we placed in our channelMap.

Notice the area named "Destination Mappings" off to the right. We can scroll to the bottom of this, where we'll find variables that have been created in the channelMap. We can click and drag first_name into our template. (The syntax that appears in the template is ${first_column}, but let's not worry about that for the moment.)

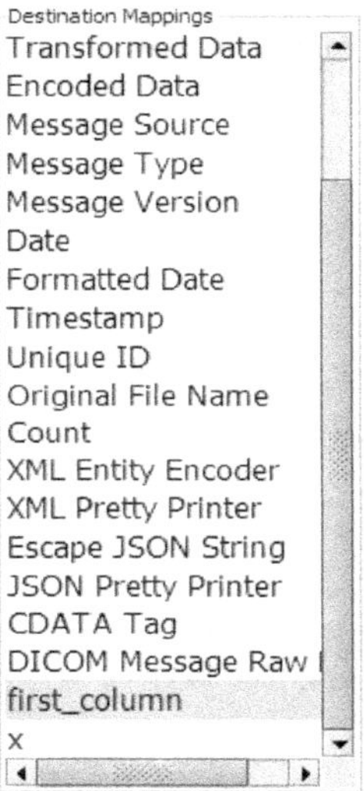

We'll add a bit of text to the template:

```
First column dragged in had: ${first_column}
```

We can now save (Channel Tasks/Save Changes) and deploy (Channel Tasks/Deploy Channel) our channel, highlight it in the Dashboard window, and once again send it a "Hello, Mirth!" (Dashboard Tasks/Send Message).

With the channel highlighted in the dashboard, we can choose Dashboard Tasks/View Messages or select View Messages from the popup which appears when we right click over the channel's row, then click on the Destination of message 2 and inspect the different versions. The "Sent" radio button shows the following:

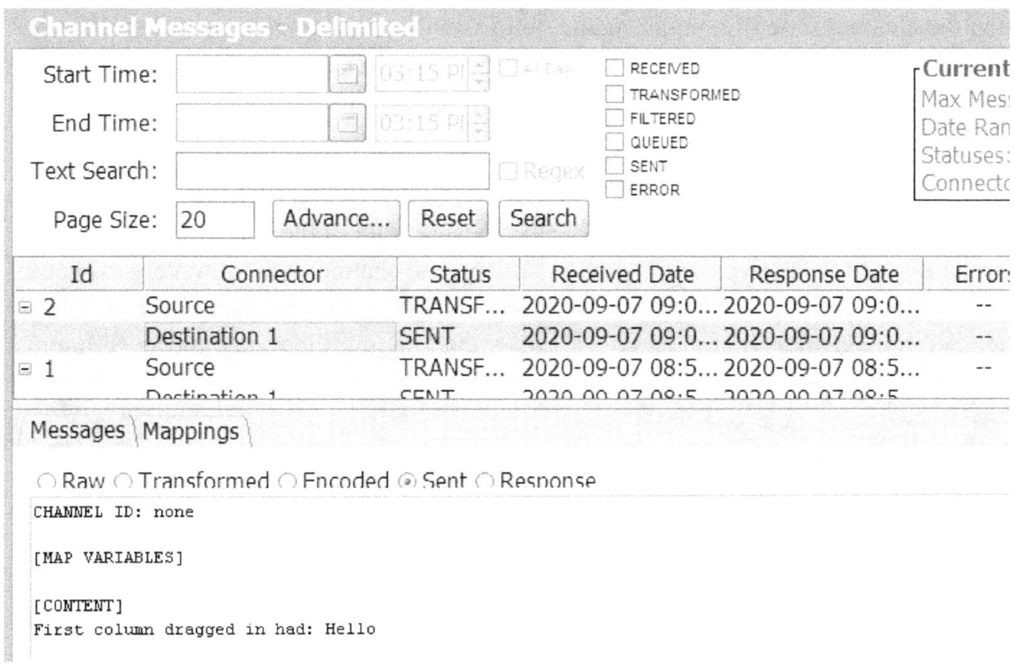

The channel has stored the map values that were in effect when the message was sent, and you can click over from the Messages tab to the Mappings tab to see that there was a value first_column in the channelMap (Scope: Channel) whose value was "Hello." Also notice that there is a response stored in the channel.

Building a "Drag and Drop" Transformer

OK, this was ugly and, if you aren't used to programming, probably a bit intimidating. Mirth attempts to provide simpler mechanisms to accomplish these tasks via the user interface, and we'll look at that now. But, particularly if you are familiar with programming, I can guarantee you that it will pay you to understand what Mirth is doing under the hood when you use the interface, because there will be times when the results only make sense if you understand how the messages appear as XML, and how Mirth deals with that XML.

Let's do this once again, this time aided by the user interface.

Open the channel for editing once again, go to the Source tab, and select Channel Tasks/Edit Transformer (1). Disable the step you created earlier by clicking in the Enabled column to uncheck the checkbox. Then, select Transformer Tasks/Add New Step.

In the area on the right, click on "Message Templates" to select that tab. In the box that accepts an inbound message template, we'll type a sample of the sort of message this channel expects to receive. For example, perhaps the channel will ultimately expect to get three fields on each spreadsheet row; we could enter "one, two, three" or "a, b, c" or, if we have an existing file, we can read it in by clicking the file folder and selecting that file.

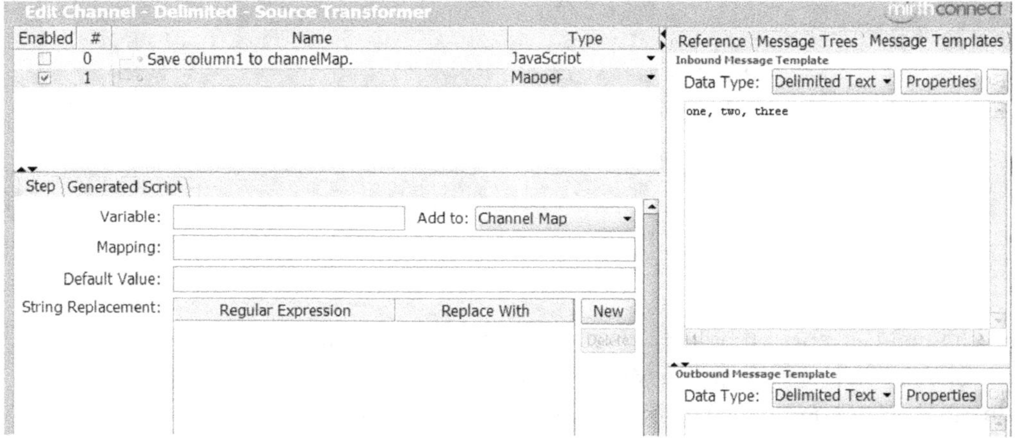

Now, at the top, select the "Message Trees" tab. Mirth shows a tree-style view of the XML that it creates when "one, two, three," our template, is received as delimited text. You can expand a node of the tree by clicking on the boxed plus sign(s).

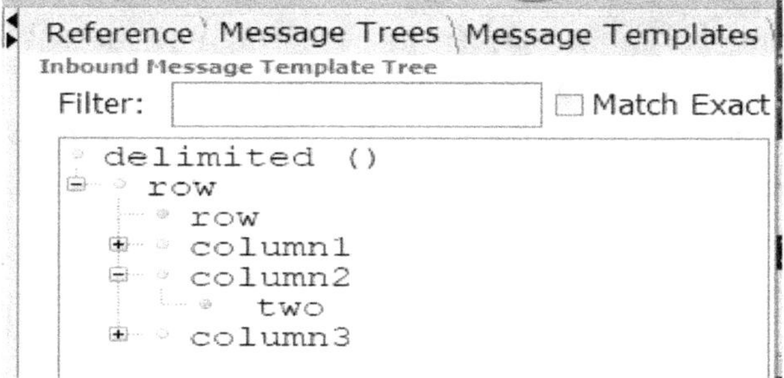

Let's say we want to work with the part of the CSV message following the first comma -- what Mirth has labeled "column 2." Drag the word "two" from its place in the tree over to the empty field labeled "Mapping" and Mirth will convert it to the code needed to access the corresponding text from a message: msg['row']['column2'].toString(). In the variable field, type the name "second_column." As you do so, you'll notice that in the area above where you are typing, this variable name is entered as the name of the transformer, which is of type "Mapper."

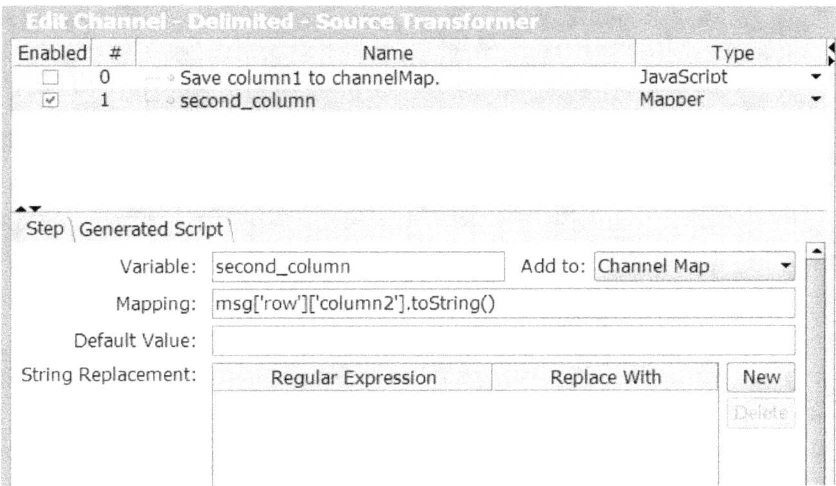

What's critical here is that even if you choose not to use the Mirth drag-and-drop UI when you are more comfortable with Mirth, the Message Template area provides you with a good reference to the Javascript that does its tasks; the center lower window has two tabs, and you can see the Javascript Mirth will use by clicking on "Generated Script." First, we can add a default value to use, in case there is no second field on a CSV row:

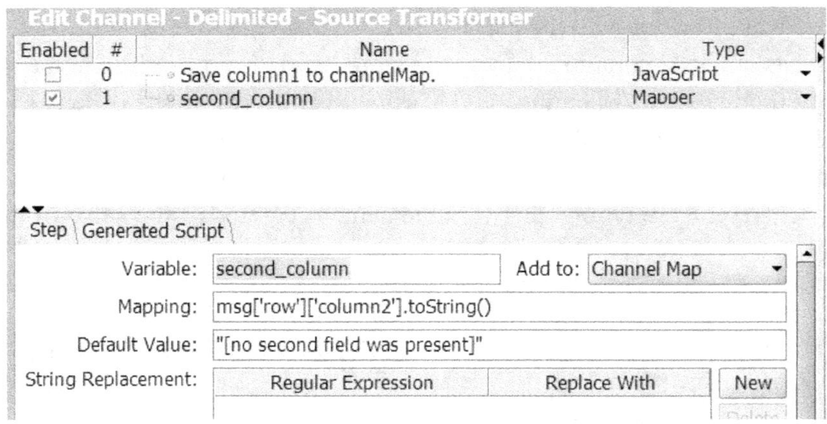

And then we can click over to the "Generated Script" tab:

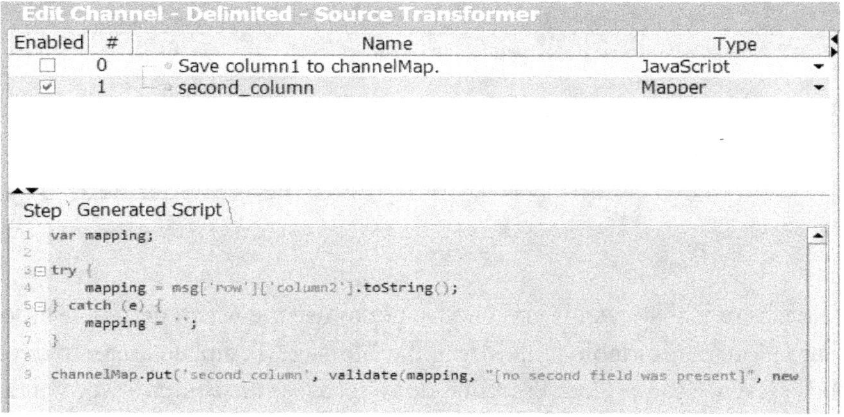

The generated script, like what we entered earlier manually, creates a variable and stores part of the message into it, then stores that value into the channelMap, under the name we've specified. The generated code also handles providing a default value to be used if none was present in an incoming message.

In many situations, you will want to generate a complete new message out of the spreadsheet data. For now, notice that there is also an outbound message template area, and we could, for example, change our outbound data type to HL7 and read a template for our desired HL7 message structure into that area. We could then drag from the inbound template to the outbound template to build our message. But that's getting ahead of ourselves.

Let's set up our destination connector to use the second_column variable from the channelMap. We select Mirth Connect Views/Back to Channel, then click on the Destinations tab, and once again scroll to the bottom of the Destination Mappings area on the right. It now contains the field second_column, and we can drag that into our channel writer Template field:

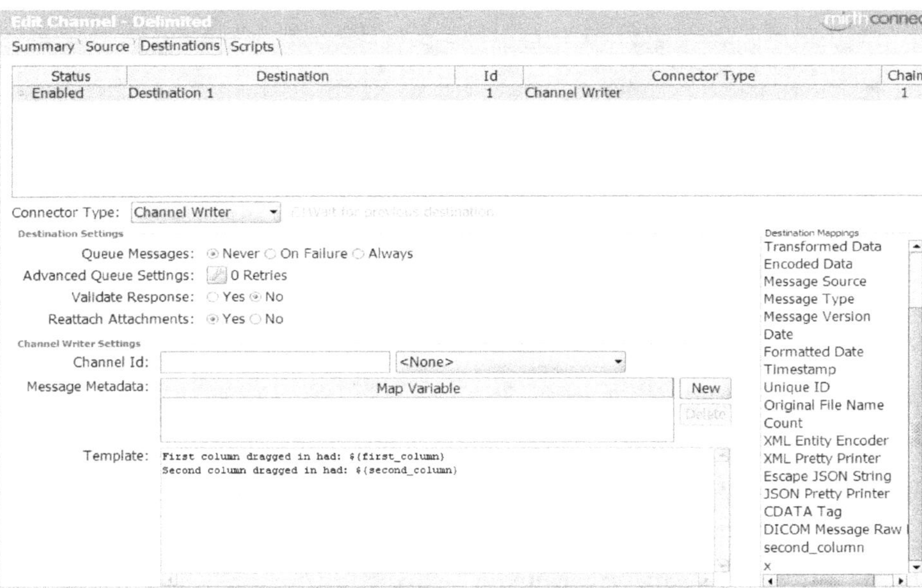

If we want to see our first column as well, we'll need to reenable our manual transformer by rechecking its "Enabled" checkbox on the Source connector's transformer view. Save the channel and deploy it. From the Dashboard, send it the message "Hello, Mirth, how are you? Then examine the resulting message sent by the destination:

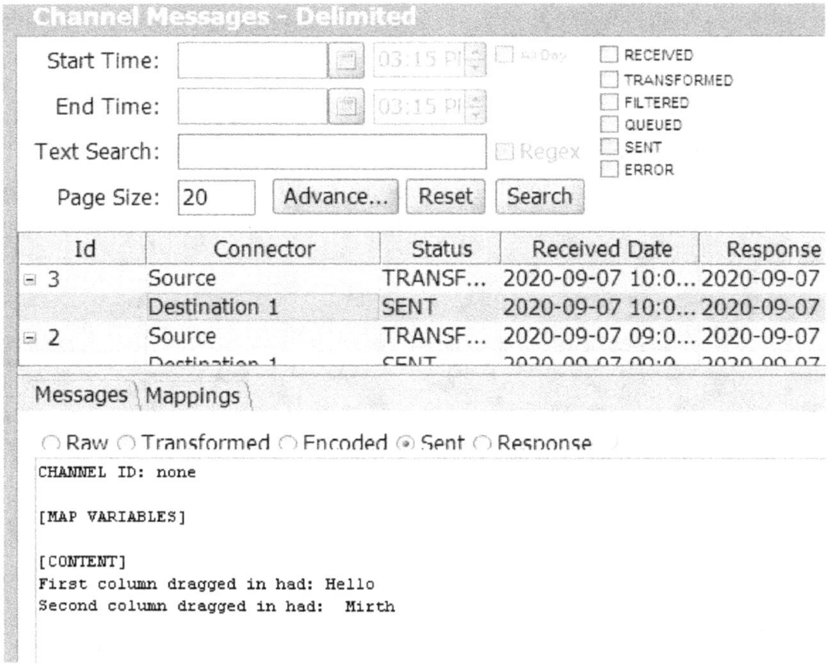

Channel Messages - Delimited

Start Time: 03:15 PM All Day

End Time: 03:15 PM

Text Search: Regex

Page Size: 20 Advance... Reset Search

RECEIVED
TRANSFORMED
FILTERED
QUEUED
SENT
ERROR

Id	Connector	Status	Received Date	Response
3	Source	TRANSF...	2020-09-07 10:0...	2020-09-07
	Destination 1	SENT	2020-09-07 10:0...	2020-09-07
2	Source	TRANSF...	2020-09-07 09:0...	2020-09-07

Messages Mappings

Raw Transformed Encoded Sent Response

```
CHANNEL ID: none

[MAP VARIABLES]

[CONTENT]
First column dragged in had: Hello
Second column dragged in had:  Mirth
```

From the Dashboard view, select Destination 1 of the message. The Raw version of the data is what you typed, “Hello, Mirth, how are you?” The Transformed and Encoded versions show the XML that resulted. The Sent view shows that it was your template that was sent, not the original message.

What happens if we send a message with no second column, like “Hello Mirth!”

Try it. If you entered a default value in our Mapper transformer, that value will appear in the Sent version of the Destination message:

```
[CONTENT]

First column dragged in had: Hello Mirth!

Second column dragged in had: [no second field was present]
```

Let's pause for a moment to soak in this victory, because this is where we come to the first Mirth boobytrap (and the reason we are starting with CSV data rather than HL7).

Most spreadsheets have more than one record, don’t they? Let’s send two lines of CSV data:

```
alpha1, alpha2, alpha3
beta1, beta2, beta3
```

The transformed version looks like this:

```
<delimited>
    <row>
        <column1>alpha1</column1>
        <column2> alpha2</column2>
        <column3> alpha3</column3>
    </row>
    <row>
        <column1>beta1</column1>
        <column2> beta2</column2>
        <column3> beta3</column3>
    </row>
</delimited>
```

But our sent value now looks like this:

```
[CONTENT]
First column dragged in had:
<column1>alpha1</column1><column1>beta1</column1>
Second column dragged in had: <column2>
alpha2</column2><column2> beta2</column2>
```

What's going on?!

Mirth, internally, uses a library called E4X (ECMAScript for XML). When you write a Javascript expression like msg['row']['column2'].toString(), E4X will return the contents of a node, but will return a text representation of the XML if there was a list of items.

This is only horrible if you don't know it is going to happen. Now you know it is going to happen. For spreadsheet data, we can avoid this by treating each line of the spreadsheet as a separate message for processing purposes. It's a simple fix to our channel, just turning on "Process Batch" in our Source tab:

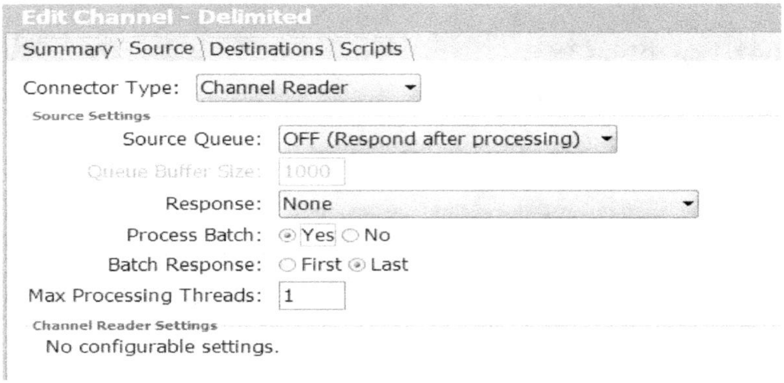

Edit Channel - Delimited
Summary | Source | Destinations | Scripts
Connector Type: Channel Reader
Source Settings
Source Queue: OFF (Respond after processing)
Queue Buffer Size: 1000
Response: None
Process Batch: Yes No
Batch Response: First Last
Max Processing Threads: 1
Channel Reader Settings
No configurable settings.

Once we tell our channel to process incoming messages as batches, then save and redeploy our channel, it can receive a multiple line message, like a real spreadsheet, and process each line independently. Sending a two line message once again, this time with lines “a,b,c” and “d,e,f”, creates two messages; the first using the first line and the second using the second line as its source.

When working with HL7, there are many situations where parts of a message might have multiple sub-entries. Worse, there are situations in which an early HL7 version expects one item but later versions accept multiple versions in the same location. One straightforward example is a patient’s name. In the field for a patient’s name, there may be a legal name, a nickname, a so-called maiden name, and so on. If you expect to see something like “SMITH, JANE”, you may be surprised to suddenly see XML instead, when you encounter a field that repeats.

Without spending too much time on this issue, I’ll just mention that the solution here is to write Javascript that will test for multiple items and process all of them (“iterating over a list” is the programmers’ expression). If you want to work further on the CSV examples, you could delete your “mapper” transformer and replace it with a Javascript transformer with code like this:

```
var repeats = 0;
var channel_string = 'Second column entries are ';
repeats = msg['row'].length();
for (x=0; x < repeats; x++){
    channel_string += ',' + msg['row'][x]
['column2'].toString()
```

```
}
channelMap.put('test_extract',channel_string.substring(1));
```

If you disable batch processing, save, redeploy, and send a two line message again, the result will be a channelMap entry named "test_extract" with the value "Second column entries are alpha2, beta2"

Recent versions of Mirth include iteration in the user interface. I find it easiest to write Javascript for such situations but you may disagree. You will find a step by step discussion in the Mirth User Guide.

We'll go into more detail on this in the HL7 sections, but you can also assign to message fields in transformers -- they are called "transformers," after all. Use an assignment statement like this, as long as there is only one instance of SEG.n.m in the entire message:

```
msg['SEG']['SEG.n']['SEG.n.m'] = 'text value';
```

An important note about transformers:

Keep in mind that transformers used in source and destination connectors are typically executed as each message goes by. If you have channel setup code that only needs to be executed once, then the better place for that code is in the channel's Deployment Script. Scripts to execute when a channel is deployed and/or undeployed can be entered on the Scripts tab, to the right of the Source and Destinations tab. You can also enter pre- and post-processing scripts which will be executed for each message.

Reading and Writing Files

So far, we haven't actually sent anything anywhere. Before we leave Delimited Text, let's connect up a channel that will read and write files.

In the Channels view, select the Delimited channel. Then select Channel Tasks/Clone Channel and, in the popup which is presented, enter a name of DelimitedFile for your cloned channel:

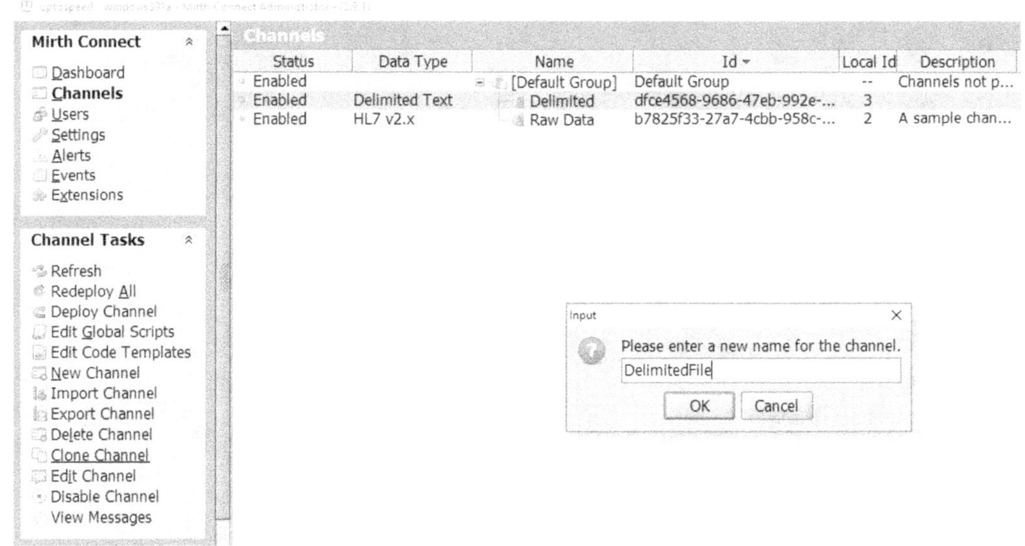

Select the Delimited channel and edit it. Go to the destinations tab. You have your one destination, which is now a Channel Writer. Change it to a File Writer by clicking on the Channel Writer option button and selecting File Writer from the dropdown.

Open the new channel, DelimitedFile, click to the Source tab, and change the source connector type from Channel Reader to File Reader. Where Channel Reader had few settings, File Reader has several.

Scheduling File Reads

You can choose how often and when you'd like to check for the file to see if it can be read.

By default, the file reader's Schedule Type is set to interval, and it checks for the file every five seconds. But you can change the schedule type to Time, for example, and specify a daily time. By clicking on the wrench icon, you can open a popup which allows you to specify that the check take place only on certain days of the week or monthly on a particular day.

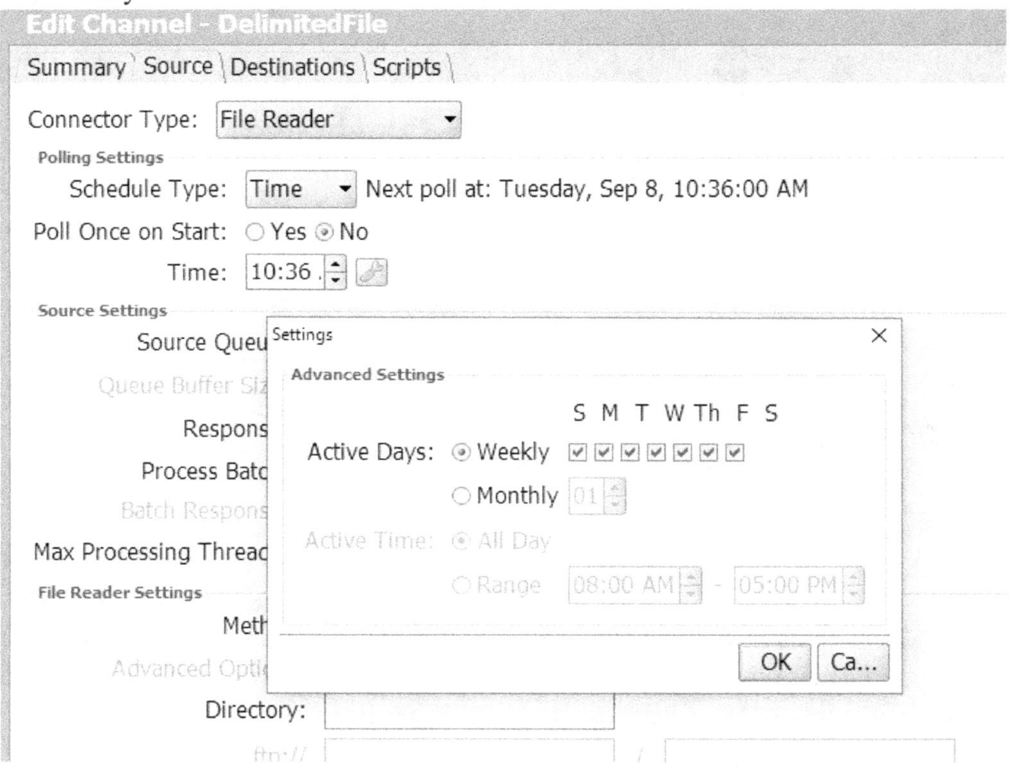

Cron expressions must be in Quartz format with at least 6 fields.

Format:

Field	Required	Values	Special Characters
Seconds	YES	0-59	, - * /
Minutes	YES	0-59	, - * /
Hours	YES	0-23	, - * /
Day of Month	YES	1-31	, - * ? / L W
Month	YES	1-12 or JAN-DEC	, - * /
Day of Week	YES	1-7 or SUN-SAT	, - * ? / L #
Year	NO	empty, 1970-2099	, - * /

Special Characters:

***** : all values
? : no specific value
- : used to specify ranges
, : used to specify list of values
/ : used to specify increments
L : used to specify the last of
W : used to specify the nearest weekday
: used to specify the nth day of the month

Example: 0 */5 8-17 * * ? means to fire every 5 minutes starting at 8am and ending at 5pm everyday

Note: Support for specifying both a day-of-week and day-of-month is not yet supported. A ? must be used in one of these fields.

There is even more flexibility available by setting the Schedule Type to "Cron," and specifying download times using a syntax that will be familiar to UNIX or Linux programmers from the cron program. Conveniently, if you switch to "Cron" and click and hover over the default entry in "Cron Jobs," Mirth pops up the syntax it uses for cron specifications.

For more information, simply search online using the search term "cron syntax." One useful site for familiarizing yourself with cron may be https://crontab.guru, but there is a wealth of information online.

By default, the channel uses the method "file," meaning it will look for files that match the filename filter you specify in the local directory you specify. You can enter a directory and filename filter in the "File Reader Settings" area. In this example, I'd like to batch process any file in C:/temp whose name begins mirth and ends csv. The files will be read and processed according to the schedule you've set up. Following processing, each file can be renamed or moved by setting the "After Processing Action" to Move or Delete. If you wish to move the files, you can drag useful names or name parts into the Move-to Directory and Move-to File Name text areas, which become available once you change the After Processing Action to Move.

File Reader Settings

Method: file | Test Read
Advanced Options: <None>
Directory: C:/temp
ftp:// /
Filename Filter Pattern: mirth*.csv ☐ Regular Expression
Include All Subdirectories: ○ Yes ⦿ No
Ignore . files: ⦿ Yes ○ No
Anonymous: ⦿ Yes ○ No
Username: anonymous
Password: •••••••••
Timeout (ms): 10000
Secure Mode: ⦿ Yes ○ No
Passive Mode: ⦿ Yes ○ No
Validate Connection: ⦿ Yes ○ No
After Processing Action: Mo...
Move-to Directory: C:/temp
Move-to File Name: ${originalFilename}.processed
Error Reading Action: No...
Error in Response Action: After Processin...
Error Move-to Directory:
Error Move-to File Name:

channelName
channelId
DATE
COUNT
UUID
SYSTIME
originalFilename

For example, the settings above search the C:/temp folder for files prefixed with "mirth" and ending with ".csv" and then rename them with the extension ".processed" so that mirth1.csv is processed once, then renamed to mirth1.csv.processed, a name which no longer satisfies the filter.

Other settings allow you to specify what to do with the file in the event of an error reading it, to require that a file have existed for a certain period (to prevent reading partially written files), and to change the order in which they are processed.

In addition to local files, you are able to use ftp (file transfer protocol) and sftp (secure file transfer protocol), smb (session message block) and webdav (web distributed authoring and versioning, but, really, just webdav) as sources of files.

Depending on the file source you use, different configuration options become available, both in the source tab and by clicking the wrench to the right of your selected Method. For example, to retrieve files using sftp, you might need to present a passphrase protected "key file" in order to prove you have rights to connect and retrieve your file. Once you've set the method to sftp, you can click the wrench icon to open a popup dialog to enter this information:

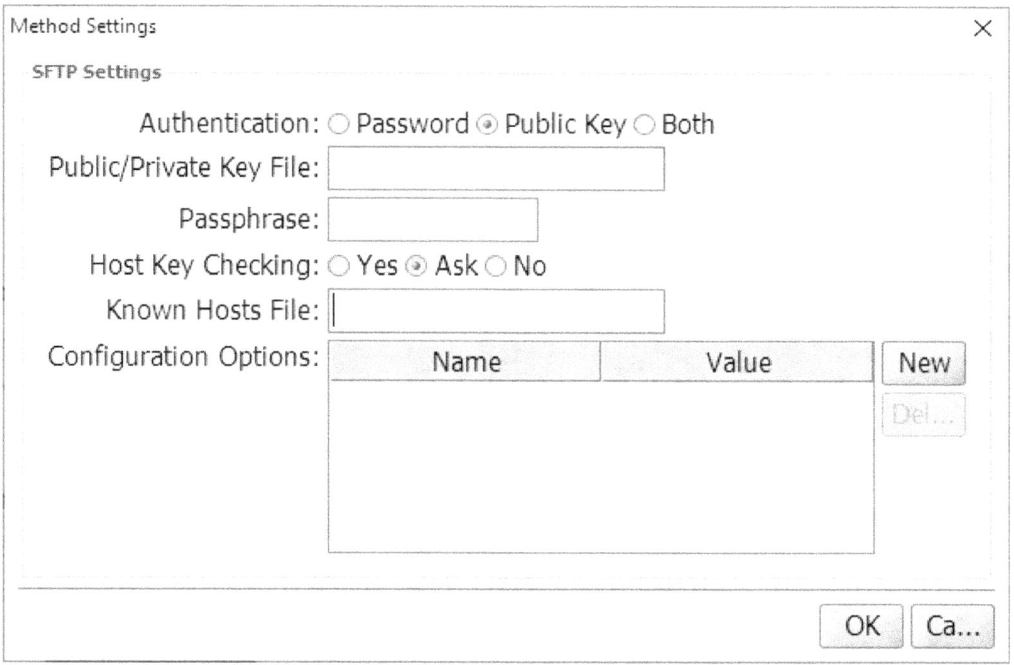

Please note that the information you enter becomes part of your channel, and is exported when you export your channel to XML. There are ways of forcing exports to be encrypted, or instead of entering text, you can use special map variables which can be retrieved from a protected file when Mirth starts up.

(Beware of using channel name; it can change over time. The channel id will not.)

Writing to Files

To write to a file, or to send it by ftp or webdav or some other mechanism, create a Destination Connector of type File Writer.

Once again, you have a choice of sending to the local filesystem, or using ftp, sftp, Amazon S3, smb, or webdav protocols. You can drag variables from the "Destination Mappings" area on the right into the File or Directory fields, and can mix the variables with text.

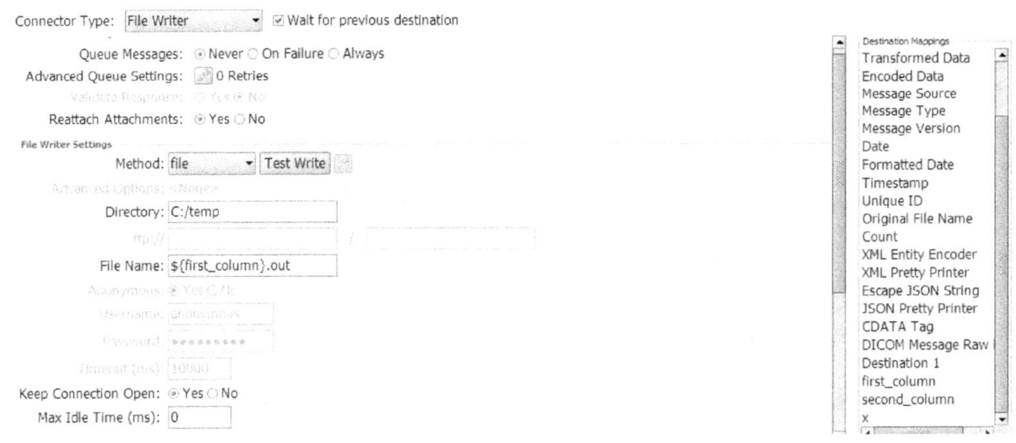

In the settings above, we are using the first_column information stored by the source connector to generate the first part of our output filename, and then we append the suffix ".out" The ${first_column} is substituted with the value of the channelMap variable first_column, by a templating engine named Velocity.

This templating engine is also often the source of the information sent by the channel, which appears in the Message Template area. Dragging "Encoded Data" from the area on the right into the Message Template will populate it with a Velocity substitution -- ${message.encodedData} – which is the message's encoded form.

“$” Velocity substitutions

There are several different sets of variables available to your channel. Many of these are in various maps that are available at different stages of a message's lifecycle.

These maps include the channelMap, which we've seen, where variables are available to all the connectors for one message's processing. In addition, there is the connectorMap, where the variable is only available to one connector for one message; the globalChannelMap and globalMap, where the variable is available for processing of all messages in a channel (globalChannelMap) or any channel (globalMap), or where configuration information from your Mirth install is stored (configurationMap). Typically, this will be in the appdata subfolder of your Mirth installation, in a file named configuration.properties (e.g., on Windows, C:\Program Files\Mirth Connect\appdata\ configuration.properties). To edit it, you may need to temporarily rename the file to configuration_properties.txt, open it with a plain text editor like Notepad on Windows, and then rename it to configuration.properties. For more information on these and other maps, go to the “Variable Map” section of Mirth's user guide.

There is an abbreviated form for setting and getting information from these maps. Instead of channelMap.put('varname','varvalue'), you can say instead $c('varname','varvalue'). Instead of channelMap.get('varname'), you can say $c('varname').

There is also an abbreviated form for looking through all maps: ${varname}.

The search sequence is ResponseMap ($r), ConnectorMap ($co), ChannelMap ($c), SourceMap ($s), GlobalChannelMap ($gc), GlobalMap ($g), ending with ConfigurationMap ($cfg). When a variable is first encountered in a map during the lookup process, its value from that map is substituted and the search concludes.

For more information about Velocity templating in general, you can check out the home of the Apache Velocity Project, https://velocity.apache.org.

Switching to a Production Ready Database

We've now seen some basics, and even some not-so-basics, of how Mirth operates. Before we go any further, this would be a good point to switch from the built in Derby database backend to a database that we could continue to use in production. Since PostgreSQL is a mature and robust open source database, we'll switch to that.

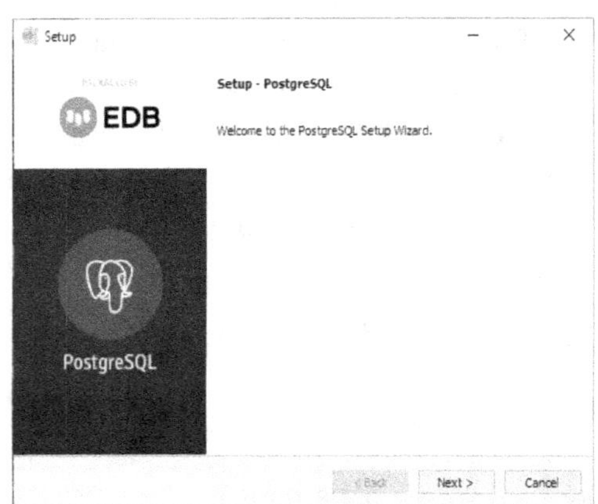

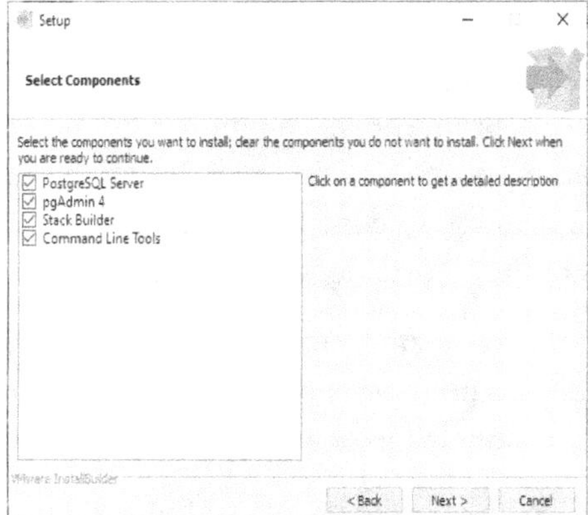

You can download the most recent version of PostgreSQL for Windows, Macs, and Linux (as well as Solaris and BSD) from https://www.postgresql.org/download/. For Windows and MacOS, the download link gets you an interactive installer that lets you install not just PostgreSQL but also pgAdmin, a graphic interface for interacting with Postgres, and a current JDBC (Java Database Connectivity) driver.

Following a Windows install of PostgreSQL, you may need to restart. When you do, you will have a Postgres submenu in your Start menu, and PostgreSQL's GUI, pgAdmin4, will be an option in that menu.

If you are using Linux, install Postgres and pgAdmin via your Linux package management tools. Check the download pages at https://www.postgresql.org for information specific to your distribution.

Using pgAdmin4, you'll need to connect to your local PostgreSQL and create a new database named "mirthdb" and belonging to PostgreSQL's default user, "postgres". Just open pgAdmin4, click on Server to expand it, and right-click on Databases to choose "Create" "Database..."

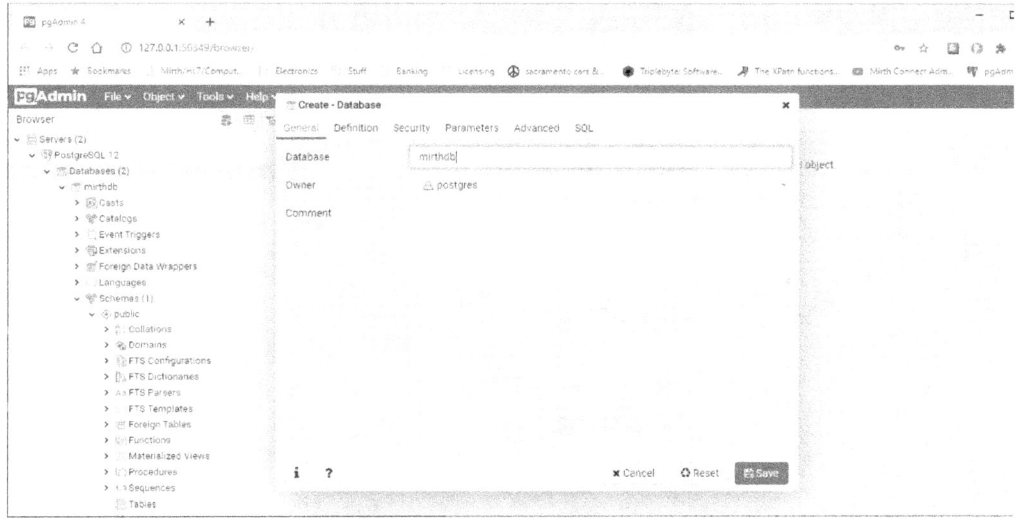

You just need to create the database; Mirth itself will set up tables when it first uses the database you've created.

(Note that Postgres DB ports shown in some diagrams are non default. If you are installing a first instance of Postgres DB, use the default ports suggested in the install.)

If you would like to save your existing work, you can do a complete backup of your Mirth configuration now. Using the Administrator, you would go to the Settings tab using the first menu block on the left side, and then select "Backup Config" from the second menu block, "Server Tasks," on the left side. This will give you an XML file which you can then import into the new database, using "Restore Config" after you've completed your switchover.

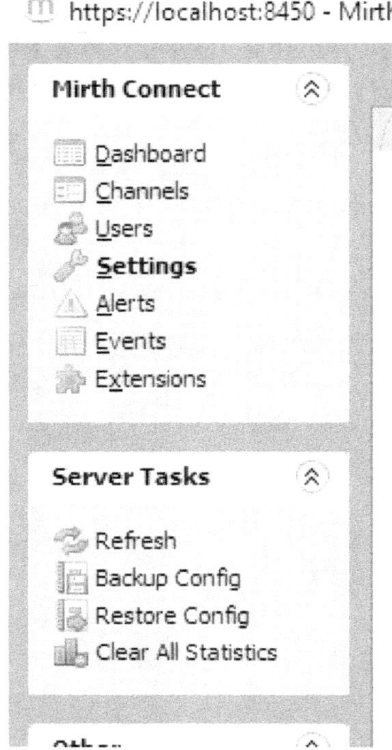

(Note: Switching to another database will not cause your Derby database to disappear. If, at some later point, you switch Mirth back to use Derby, it will pick up where it left off in Derby.)

Back to switching; use the Mirth Server Manager to stop your running Mirth process, if any, and go to its Database tab, which, unless you've changed it, will show the connection to the default database backend that ships with Mirth, Derby:

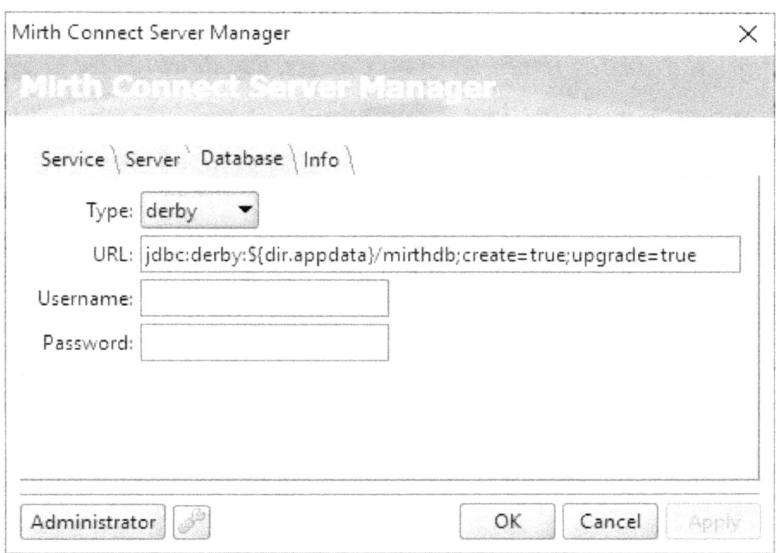

Change your connection type in the Type dropdown to Postgres:

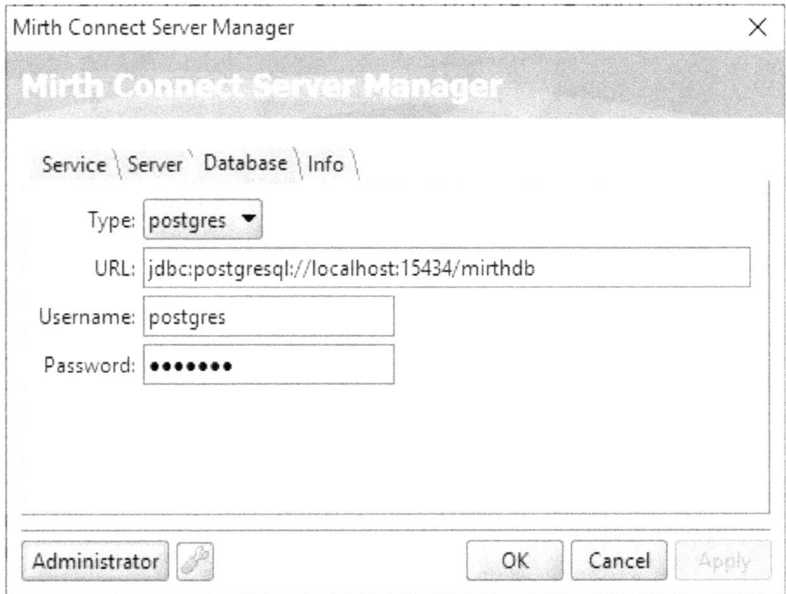

(Note that the normal port following "localhost:"would be 5432; use the port you assigned PostgreSQL during the installation process, which will be 5432 by default.)

Assuming you have just followed the instructions from earlier, and now have an empty database named mirthdb, belonging to postgres, use the username postgres and the password you assigned to PostgreSQL's postgres user when you did your PostgreSQL installation. Click OK in the server manager's database tab, and switch to the Service tab and restart your Mirth server. After it has run for a minute, you can check back in pgAdmin4 to see that Mirth has created some tables:

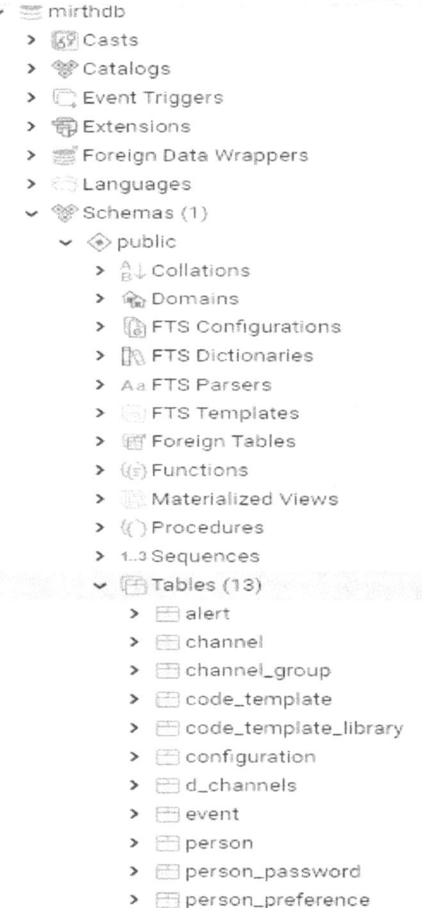

An HL7v2 channel

We've now seen some basics, and even some not-so-basics, of how Mirth operates. Before we send messages to a TCP/IP destination, let's switch gears and start using HL7. This seems like the time to do that, because we will soon begin examining message responses, and HL7 defines what successful responses must look like.

Your existing channels are still available in the Derby database. If you want to, you can switch back to the Derby database, or you can restore the configuration you saved prior to switching databases, which will create the necessary tables in Postgres.

Regardless of which way you proceed, you never want to use Derby as your production database.

Setting up HAPI TestPanel

While it's not strictly necessary, I'd strongly suggest that before you proceed you download one of the several free non-Mirth tools available for sending and receiving HL7 messages. A good choice would be the HAPI Test Panel from https://sourceforge.net/projects/hl7api/files/hapi-testpanel/

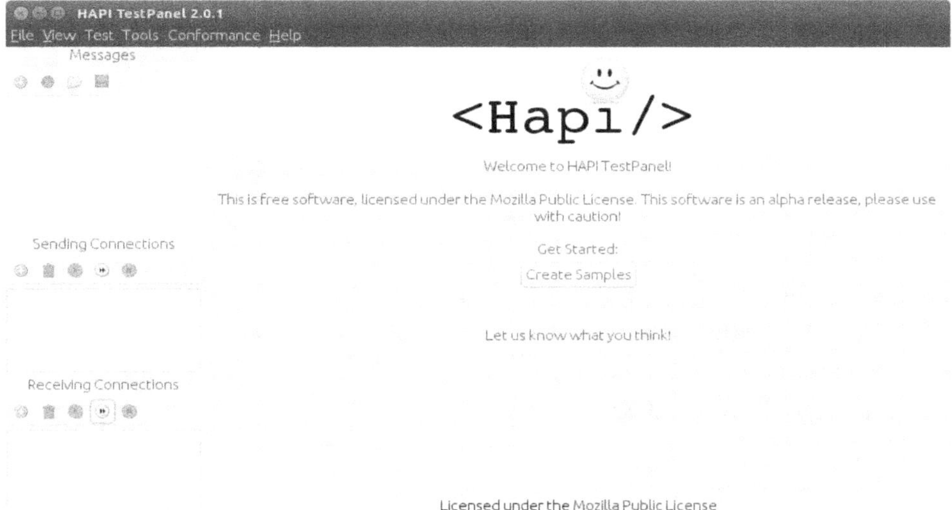

From the menu, select Test > Populate TestPanel with sample messages and connections. It will then look like this (port numbers will vary, as they are chosen at random).

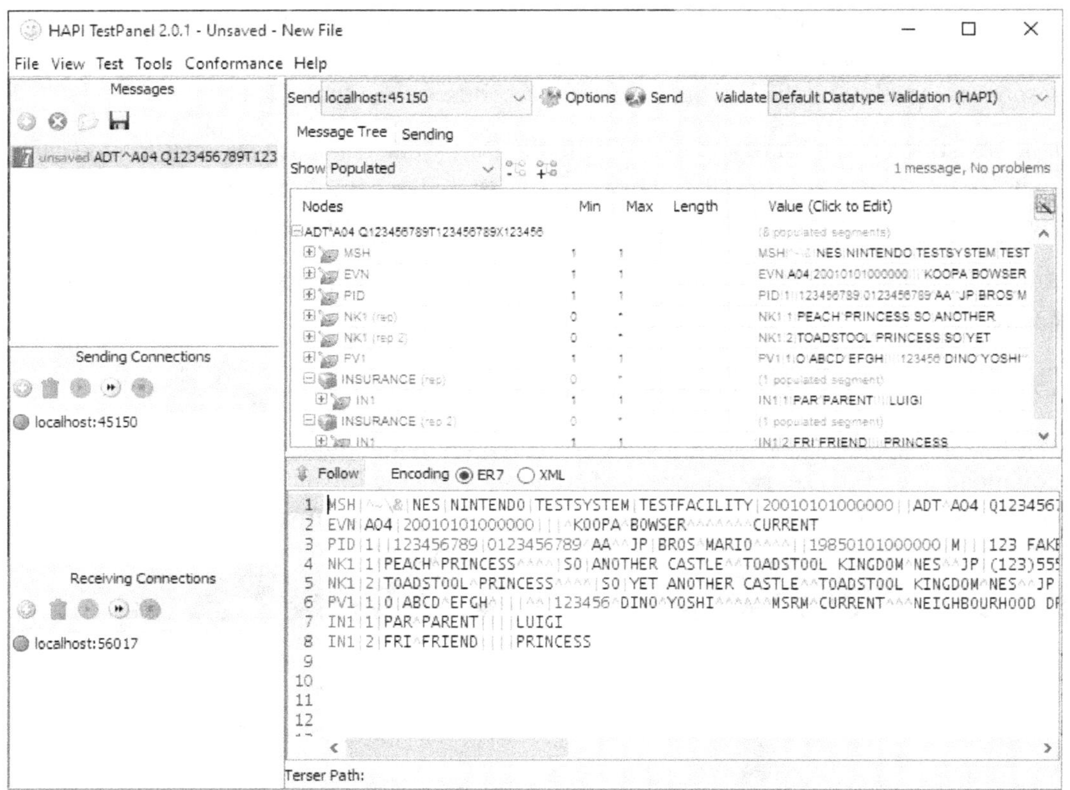

We'll do a quick overview of HL7 in the next chapter; for now, it's enough to know that we have a message loaded into the editing area at lower right, and we can create sending connections in the Sending Connections area at left. That gives us the ability to send an HL7 message from HAPI Test Panel into the listening Mirth channel we'll now create.

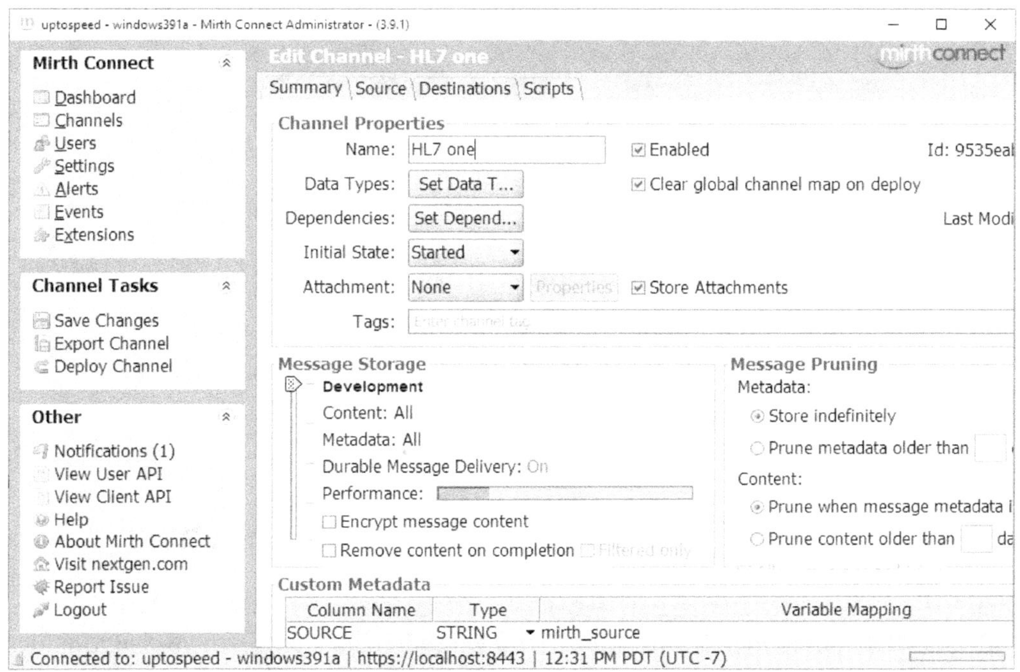

Back in Mirth, select the Channels view and select Channel Tasks/New Channel. On the summary tab, we'll name the channel HL7 one, and give it a small description.

Using a TCP Listener

The default connector defined on the Source tab is ChannelReader. We'll change it to TCP Listener. We can go with all default values except one: we'll change the port on which we'll listen for messages to the port which HAPI chose at random, in this case 45150.

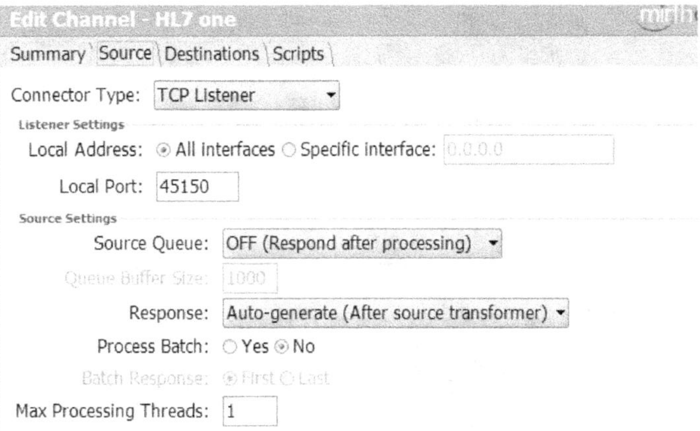

An HL7 TCP/IP Receiver, A Mirth-Generated Response

HAPI test panel randomly selected port 45150 to send on, so that's what we've filled in on our new channel as our port to listen for messages on. We'll save our channel and deploy it.

At the top of the HAPI Test Panel, when we highlight the test message on the left, we get a green send button at the upper top of the screen. We'll click it to send that message to Mirth and see what happens.

On the HAPI Test Panel, the central area now shows a sequence of an outgoing message, a connection attempt, a connection success, and a response. Mirth has automatically generated an HL7 response to indicate that it has received the message.

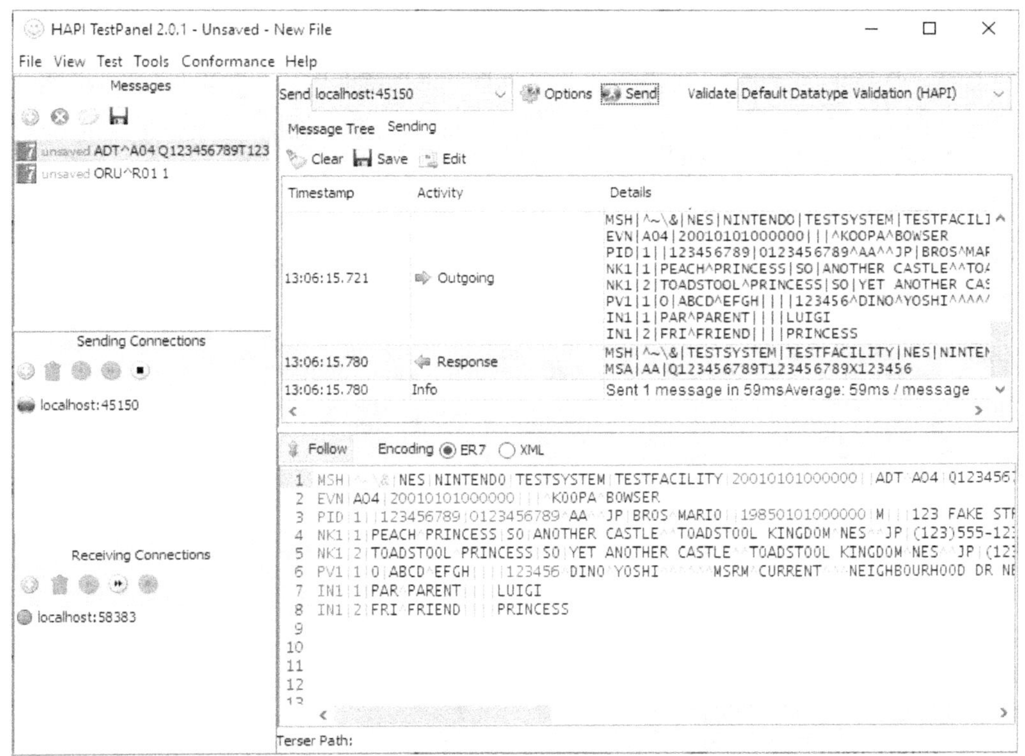

Let's look at our Mirth dashboard:

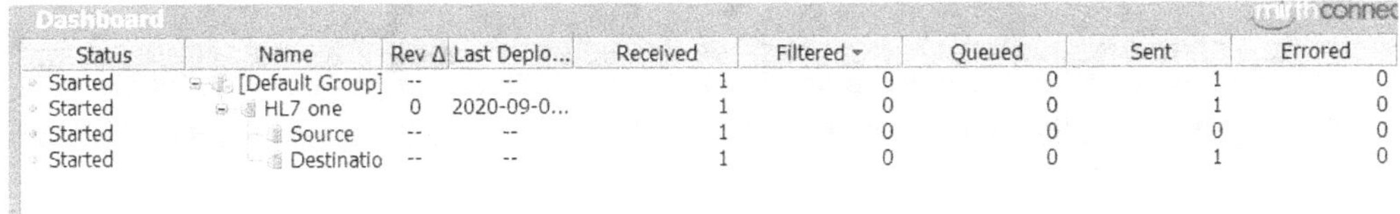

Status	Name	Rev Δ	Last Deplo...	Received	Filtered	Queued	Sent	Errored
Started	[Default Group]	--	--	1	0	0	1	0
Started	HL7 one	0	2020-09-0...	1	0	0	1	0
Started	Source	--	--	1	0	0	0	0
Started	Destinatio	--	--	1	0	0	1	0

Mirth has now received one message on HL7 one, and has sent it onwards to the channel's default destination. Right click on HL7 one, and select View messages, then highlight the message; the bottom of the screen will display the message that Mirth has received:

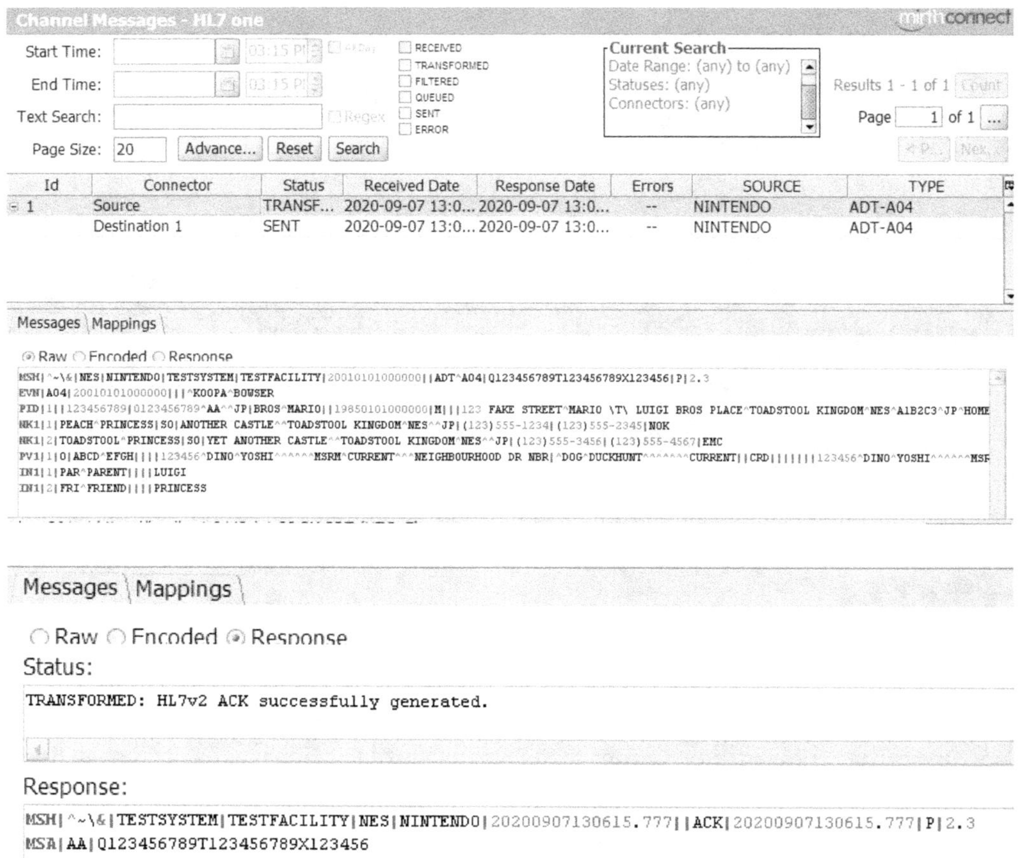

By clicking on the Response radio button, we can see the response Mirth generated and sent back to HAPI Test Panel. It's also visible in the last test panel screenshot.

Undeploy channel "HL7 one." (That's important; we don't want two channels listening to the same port.)

An HL7 transformer

We had a very brief look at a transformer when we were sending simple spreadsheet data. One thing we saw was that the transformers generally operate on an XML "serialized" version of the message. We can add a transformer to our source connector now, to extract a field from our incoming HL7 and append it to a file.

Let's clone a channel from HL7 one, using the Channel Tasks area's option "Clone channel," and name its clone "HL7 with source transformer." We'll start with an empty Javascript source transformer. Normally, a source transformer will pull out a piece of the message and perhaps manipulate it; let's just put in a dummy transformer that does nothing, in order to force Mirth to create an XML version of the message.

Edit the cloned channel's name and go to the source tab. Select Channel Tasks/Edit transformer and then Channel Tasks/Add new step. By default, the transformer type will be mapper. Double-click on the word Mapper and, in the popup, select Javascript. We can leave the Javascript transformer empty.

We can go back to the channel and save it now, and send it the same message from HAPI Test Panel that we earlier sent to HL7 one. On the Dashboard, we can see the message counts go from zero to one, and we can highlight the channel and select "View Messages" once again. Highlighting the first message in the source connector, we now have four options, "Raw,", "Transformed," "Encoded," and "Response" where before, in channel "HL7 one" we had three, "Raw," Encoded," and "Response."

If you've skipped here without looking at the earlier sections, and you are now looking at the XML in surprise, I'd strongly advise you to go back at least to where we processed a CSV style message. Mirth transforms messages into XML to allow you to refer to subparts and alter them or use them in decision-making.

The XML version of our inbound message begins like this:

```
<HL7Message>
    <MSH>
        <MSH.1>|</MSH.1>
        <MSH.2>^~\&amp;</MSH.2>
        <MSH.3>
            <MSH.3.1>NES</MSH.3.1>
        </MSH.3>
        <MSH.4>
            <MSH.4.1>NINTENDO</MSH.4.1>
```

As seen in that section, we access a particular component of a particular field in a particular segment by using a notation that refers to the intermediate nodes in the XML. The XML follows a tree structure which is shown above by indentation: MSH.4 is a branch of MSH which is a branch of HL7Message. MSH.4.1 is a leaf node that has a value of "NINTENDO" in the message above.

Let's say we want the patient's street address. There's a spot for that in the message: it is the PID segment's eleventh field's first component. In the XML tree structure, the path to the node's value is through the HL7 message node, the PID node, the PID.11 node, and the PID.11.1 node.

The syntax we use to get there in the XML is as follows:

```
msg['PID']['PID.11']['PID.11.1'].toString()
```

Although it may not be obvious why "toString()" must be included, that ensures we get back a String value as opposed to an XML value.

Perhaps we want our transformer to ensure that the word STREET is always converted to an abbreviation: ST. That can be done in one (ugly and long) line of Javascript code:

```
msg['PID']['PID.11']['PID.11.1'] = \
  msg['PID']['PID.11']['PID.11.1'].toString().replace('STREET','ST.');
```

(English translation: In the XML object msg, walk the node tree to get to the PID.11.1 node, take its value, convert it to a text string, and replace STREET with ST. in that text string. Then assign the string with replacements as the new value of the PID.11.1 node of the XML object msg.)

Editing the channel, we can go to the Source tab, choose Edit Transformer from the Tasks menu on the left, select our existing empty task, and add that string of Javascript. We'll also give the step an explanatory name:

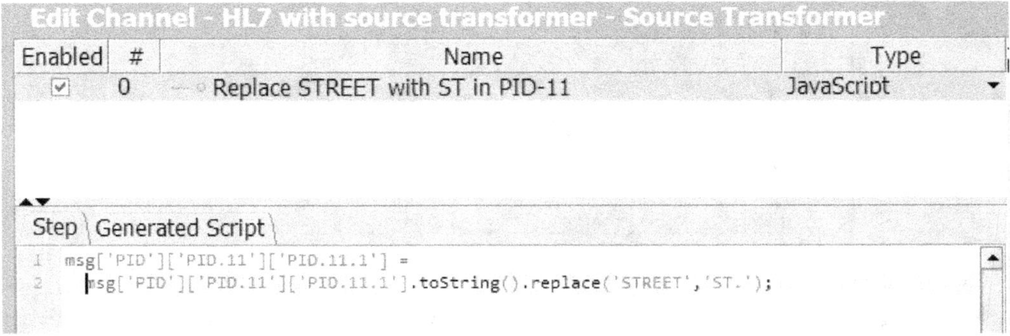

We return to the channel overview ("Back to channel") and save and deploy the channel. The old version is undeployed and replaced with the new version, and the Dashboard shows this by highlighting the "Last deployed" time for the channel.

We can now send the message again, and see what happens. The Raw version on the source connector will still show 123 FAKE STREET, but the transformed version (in XML) will show this:

```
<PID.11.1>123 FAKE ST.</PID.11.1>.
```

All subsequent versions, including those at any destination, will see the abbreviated version of the street address. Here's a fragment from the source connector's encoded version, surrounded by the delimiting pipe and hat used in HL7:

```
|123 FAKE ST.^
```

Again, Mirth includes facilities to somewhat simplify the process of generating the appropriate Javascript for tasks like this. They are explained in a fair amount of detail in the users guide, and they are helpful in many circumstances, but if you are a programmer, then in my opinion it's really important to understand that the required syntax is due to the XML nature of the stored message, and the syntax required to access the value in a particular node of XML that is accessed through the XML node tree.

If you don't track all the way to a node with a value, the toString() call will return an XML representation of the material from your node on down into the tree. For example, here is what msg['PID']['PID.11'].toString() returns, after a bit of formatting to improve readability (a/k/a prettyprinting):

```
<PID.11>
 <PID.11.1>123 FAKE STREET</PID.11.1>
 <PID.11.2>MARIO \T\ LUIGI BROS PLACE</PID.11.2>
 <PID.11.3>TOADSTOOL KINGDOM</PID.11.3>
 <PID.11.4>NES</PID.11.4>
 <PID.11.5>A1B2C3</PID.11.5>
 <PID.11.6>JP</PID.11.6>
 <PID.11.7>HOME</PID.11.7>
 <PID.11.8/>
 <PID.11.9>1234</PID.11.9>
</PID.11>
```

Also, in HL7, there can be more than one segment with the same three letter abbreviation. For example, each result in an observation message is passed as an OBX segment, and there may be a large number of OBX segments. In this case, when you request, say, the first component of the fourth field of the OBX segment, Mirth will actually return an

XML list with all of the first components of the fourth fields of all of the OBX segments. Without understanding that this is what happens, you may find yourself mystified by what comes back in your Javascript.

This same problem occurs with repeating fields within a segment, and these are not hypothetical issues. While Mirth provides an increasingly complex drag-and-drop UI to enable you to reach down into repeats, if you don't understand what you are doing beyond "dragging and dropping," you will find yourself in trouble.

Always keep in mind that Mirth "thinks" in XML, even though it may be working on CSV or regular text or the "pipe-and-hat" version of HL7 version 2.

An HL7 Sender

Every Mirth channel has a source connector and one or more destination connectors. We can send our transformed message on to new destinations, be they files, TCP/IP sockets, email addresses, or some other "thing" that can negotiate a connection with Mirth.

Because we've already seen how to send a message to a file, we've already seen the basics of setting up a connector. To send an HL7 message to a TCP/IP destination, simply add a new destination connector, select the type TCP/IP, and provide the IP and port of a listening application.

If you don't have a listening application in mind, the HAPI TestPanel will do nicely. In the area labeled "Receiving Connections," click the green plus sign. HAPI will randomly select a port to listen to. Click the "Start" button in the "Incoming Message Receiver" box and the port's label on the left will go from red to green and it will say "Listening on localhost:<the port number>, no connections."

Use that port as a destination port number within a Mirth destination connector.

We'll add one to our receiving channel's set of destinations, naming it "Send to HAPI at port 36196,", and reprocess a Message we'd sent to that channel earlier. On our new destination connector, we set the type to TCP Sender, and assign a remote address of 127.0.0.1 (which means our own machine) and a port of 36196, which HAPI is set to receive at.

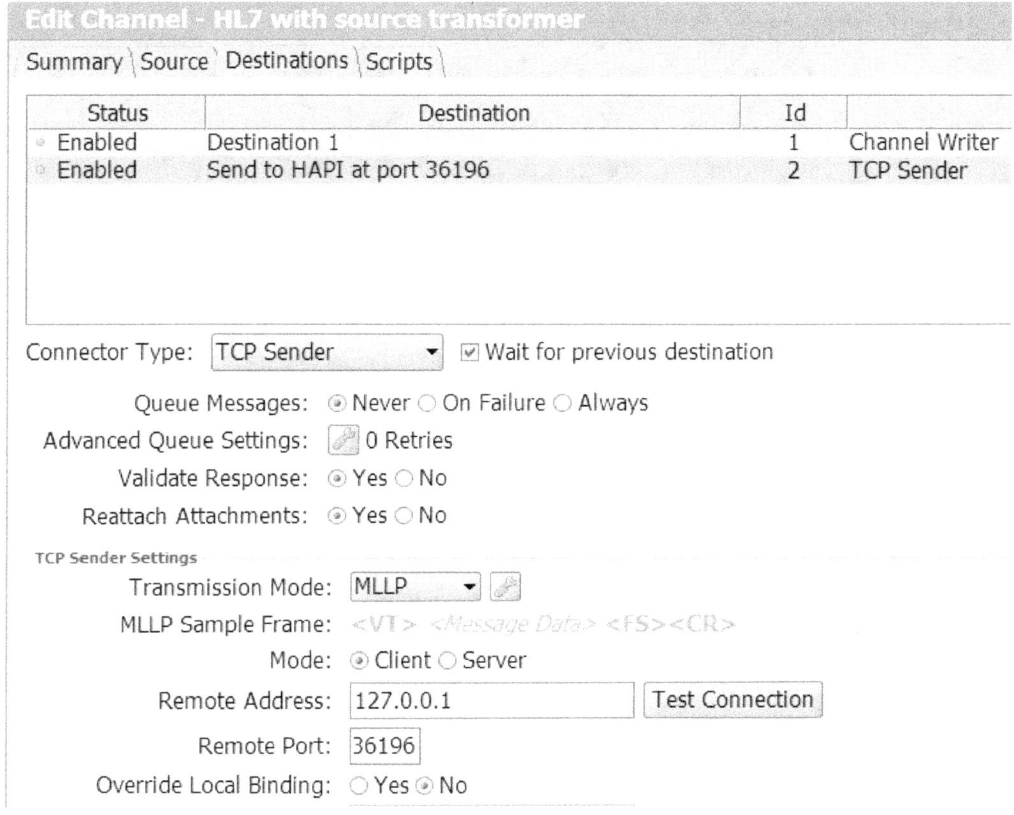

Save and (re)deploy the channel, which will take you to the Mirth Dashboard.

> (Important: if the channel does not start, is another channel listening on the port to which this channel is set to listen? If so, undeploy that other channel, and re-redeploy this one.)

Select view messages to see the messages the channel has received, and click on the source version of the last message received:

Select MessageTasks/Reprocess Message and you will be prompted as to whether you want to overwrite the message in the Mirth system, and which destinations you'd like to "reprocess." We just need to send to our new Destination, so we'll set the reprocess popup like so:

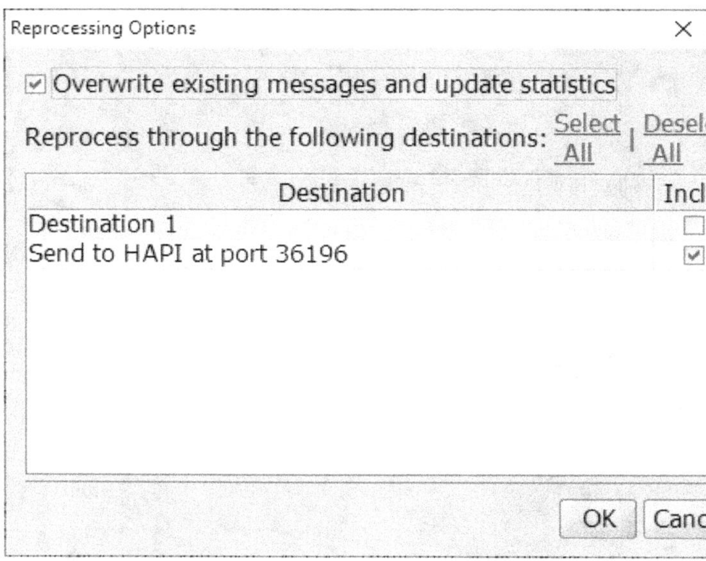

We then click OK in the popup, and perform a new search on our "Channel Messages," which will now show the message has been sent to Destination 2; selecting "Response" from the radio buttons will let us see the response sent by HAPI TestPanel.

Finally, the HAPI TestPanel now shows the message it received, and the response it sent.

Logging from Javascript

If something fails in your Javascript, you'll want, at minimum, to see how far you got. The easiest way to do this is to take advantage of Mirth's logging capability. Your Javascript code can refer to a variable named logger, with methods named error, info, warning, and debug. So adding a line like this to your Javascript:

```
logger.info('Got here')
```

will send 'Got here" to the log, as long as your logging level is set to INFO. You can control the log level from the Mirth Connect Server Manager's Server tab. Logged output lands in a folder named logs in Mirth's installation folder tree, with the most recent file named Mirth.log. You can open log files using the Mirth Connect Server Manager. In addition, the Administrator shows the most recent log lines at the bottom of its window when you are in Dashboard view.

The logging level can be configured in a file named log4j.properties in the conf subfolder of your Mirth installation (e.g., C:\Program Files\Mirth Connect\conf). This file can be edited with a text editor. (If necessary, change the file's name temporarily from log4j.properties to log4j_properties.txt, edit that in a program like Notepad, and restore it to its original name.)

Other configuration files are found in this subfolder as well as in another folder, usually named appdata, but configurable from the file mirth.properties in conf.

HL7v2: a very brief introduction

HL7 is composed of segments, which are composed of fields, which may repeat and which are composed of components. The separation between parts is done with punctuation, and generally that punctuation is the newline, the vertical pipe symbol (pipe), the carat (hat), and the tilde (squiggle). For maximum flexibility, the choice of punctuation can be changed at a particular site by changing the first few characters of the message. We will ignore that capability.

Segments are bounded by newline symbols, which are generally invisible; that means that uninterpreted messages usually appear in a text editor with one segment per line.

Segments begin with three character symbolic names: PID is short for patient identification, MSH is short for message header.

Fields are separated from one another with vertical pipe symbols "|", just as clauses in compound sentences may be separated with commas: "Mary's hat, the red one, is nice."

Components in fields are separated from one another with the caret ("hat") symbol "^", just as words in a sentence are separated by spaces.

Finally, if a field is repeated, the repeats are separated by the tilde (squiggle) character, ~.

People will refer to a specific component of a field by using index values: the patient's last name is placed in the PID-5-1; that is, the first component of the fifth field in the PID segment.

When Mirth creates an encoded representation of an HL7 message, it creates an XML structure very similar -- alas, not identical -- to what you see in HAPI TestPanel. The XML representation shows up in the "transformed" view of each message. XML is inherently tree-oriented, and as you travel from the root of the tree you refer to the segment, then the field, then the component. (If there are repeating segments, you may refer to the segment, the zero-based index of the segment instance, the field, and the component; if there are repeating fields, you may refer to the segment, the field, the zero-based index of the field instance, and the component.)

Different types of message require different sets of segments. The test message from HAPI TestPanel is an ADT (admit, discharge, transfer) message that was triggered by an event named A04 (register). This message includes:

1. an MSH segment with administrative information about the message;
2. an EVN segment for information about the event triggering the message;
3. a PID segment for information about the patient in the message;
4. two NK1 segments, each for information about one of the patient's next of kin;
5. a PV1 segment for additional information about the patient's "visit"
6. two IN1 segments for information about the patient's insurance

The segment name can be thought of as the zero-th field of the message. Segments that may be repeated will have a "set-id" field after the segment name. So, in the EVN segment, the EVN.1 field has the value A04, while in the first NK1 segment, the NK1.1 field has the "set id" value 1, the NK1.2 has the name of the next of kin: PEACH^PRINCESS. The NK1.2.1 value is PEACH, and the NK1.2.2 value is PRINCESS.

To retrieve PEACH from this message, a Mirth transformer's Javascript would be msg['NK1'][0]['NK1.2']['NK1.2.1'].toString(); we are getting the 0th NK1 segment's second field's first component.

Ugh, I know. Practice.

The meanings of the parts of a message are defined in the HL7 v2 specifications. There are many different sub-versions of HL7 v2; they are largely but not entirely backwards-compatible, and older versions are still in widespread use. There is an HL7 v3 that is not widely used, and many organizations are beginning a migration to a new standard, FHIR, right about now. HL7 v2 will likely remain in use for some time to come.

There are excellent HL7 web resources maintained as of this writing by Caristix and Corepoint Health. If you enter HL7 PID into a search engine, they will be near the top of your results. The specs themselves for the various versions are available from www.hl7.org.

Although it's not my intent to go into detail on HL7 v2, it will help us in learning Mirth to understand the basics of at least the MSH and PID segments found in most (all?) messages, and the OBR/OBX segments found in messages reporting results.

Why "HL7"?

If you are familiar with computer networking, you probably know that there is a layered approach to handle networking, with one layer worried about the physical transport of the data, a layer above that assembling the packets that go across the physical network, a layer above that handling routing of the packets, and so on. The seventh layer is the "Application Layer," and HL7 is the application layer for health applications. See, it makes sense!

MSH - Message Header

Every HL7 message starts with a header, the MSH segment. This has a few required fields and many which are optional.

The required fields, in addition to the letters MSH and the characters that can be used to break it apart (|^~\&), include the date and time of the message, the unique identifier of the message (called the message control id), the processing mode of the message (test or production, for example, with P in HAPI TestPanel's test message), and the version of HL7 to which the message conforms (2.3 in the test message)

PID - Patient Identification

The fields of a message's patient identification segment include slots for the patient's local account number along with other identifying numbers, the patient's name, date of birth, gender, mother's maiden name, address and phone number. With the exception of an identification number and a name, all fields are optional. There are also optional fields for many less obvious demographic markers, including ethnicity, race, nationality, citizenship, veteran's status.

The critical fields for basic patient identification are the PID-3, which contains the patient's internal identifying number(s), the PID-5, which contains the patient's last, first, and middle name(s), and the PID-7, which contains the patient's date of birth.

Because the online resources describe these segments in detail, I will say no more.

OBR/OBX - Observation Request, Observation and CE data type

The OBR carries numbers which uniquely identify a particular order, along with what is called a "Universal Service Id' that describes the type of observation being requested. It identifies the provider who is requesting the observation, and other providers who should be sent the observation results. In addition, it may carry information about a specimen associated with the order and, when used in reporting results, the identities of those involved in generating the results.

The OBX carries back the results of performing the requested observation. A message replying to a request for a comprehensive metabolic panel, for example, may have an OBX for each component of the panel: glucose, sodium, etc… The OBX may also carry narrative text.

It is worth taking a moment to look at the Universal Service Id. The data type of this field has evolved with HL7 version 2, but it was initially "CE," or coded entry. CE and similar data types are found not just here but throughout HL7, and they are a response to the need not just to have the name of something, but also the identity of the vocabulary from which that name came.

When we speak informally, our listeners are able to rely on a large number of contextual assumptions. For example, if I were to talk about a radio station, I might say it was 89.7. Listeners would fill in what I'd left out -- that this is an FM station that (presumably) broadcasts in my geographic location, or at least the geographic location I'd been talking about, using a modulation frequency of 89.7 megahertz. All of that is filled in automatically from context, after I've offered a number in the range of 88 to 105. If I'd instead offered a number like 630 or 1010, people would have inferred a different modulation approach (AM) and a different units for the broadcasting frequency.

Things cannot be left so informal in health care information transfer. If I'm going to refer to a test, I need to give an id for the test, an informal name for it, and the coding system that contained the id. I can also give additional ids in different coding systems. Thus, the CE data type calls for an id (an identifier, a coded value) along with a description of what is identified, and the name of the coding system that was used. For example, 2823-3 identifies "Potassium [Moles/volume] in Serum or Plasma" in a widely used coding system called LOINC. (Logical Observation Identifiers Names and Codes.)

To further identify a test, or to add convenience, it is possible to provide a second triplet of id/description/coding-system in the same CE.

More recent versions of HL7 use the CWE data type for values like Universal Service ID. CWE, or coded with exceptions, adds even more context, like the version of the coding-system. As of HL7 version 2.7, the CWE data type actually had 22 fields.

Z segments

There are many more segments defined in the HL7 standard, but I'm hopeful that these few paragraphs are enough of an introduction to help your feet touch the ground in working with HL7 in Mirth. A complete look at HL7 is beyond this guide. However, I must mention that HL7 makes allowances for carrying custom information that doesn't exactly fit with the standard segments -- this is done through segments which are named beginning with the letter Z. The information and structure of such segments are negotiated between a sender and a receiver, or groups of senders and receivers. So if you don't see a particular three letter segment name in the online resources, and the segment name begins with Z, it's been defined by its users.

Filtering Results

A single Mirth channel can have multiple destinations, and messages can be sent to any of the channel's destinations, to all of them, or to none. This is accomplished by applying filters to each destination. A filter is a bit of Javascript code which returns true if the message is to be sent to the destination with the filter, false if the message is not to be sent.

If you've done transformers with Javascript, filters are handled in just the same way. The only difference is that filters return true or false.

Filtering can also be applied to the source connector of a channel, meaning that the channel can reject incoming data if it doesn't meet your acceptance criteria. For HL7, the channel would generate a response to the sender indicating that an error had occurred with respect to handling the message.

To demonstrate filtering at destinations, we can do a channel that will look at incoming HL7 "ORU" message -- lab results -- and send all results to one destination, but only results of "complete metabolic profiles" to another channel for further processing. We'll filter the second destination on the first component of the fourth field of the first OBR segment. This is the code from the Universal Service ID of the results being returned. In an HL7 channel within Mirth, it is found as msg['OBR']['OBR.4']['OBR.4.1'].toString(). To generally understand and interpret a returned code, it's important to know what coding system was being used. That will typically be returned in the third component of the fourth field of the OBR segment, but we're going to assume that we are always looking for a code value of "CMP," and will ignore the coding system. Our filter is straightforward:

```
if (msg['OBR']['OBR.4']['OBR.4.1'].toString()=='CMP'){
 return true;
} else {
return false;
}
```

First, we create a channel named Filter Test. It is, by default, an HL7 channel, with an initial destination named Destination1. We'll leave Destination1 alone and create a new destination named CMP only. We create the channel by selecting Channel Tasks/New Channel, name it CMP only in the Summary tab, then go to the Destinations tab and

select by going to the destination tab, selecting Channel Tasks/New Destination, and double-clicking on the new destination's name to edit it:

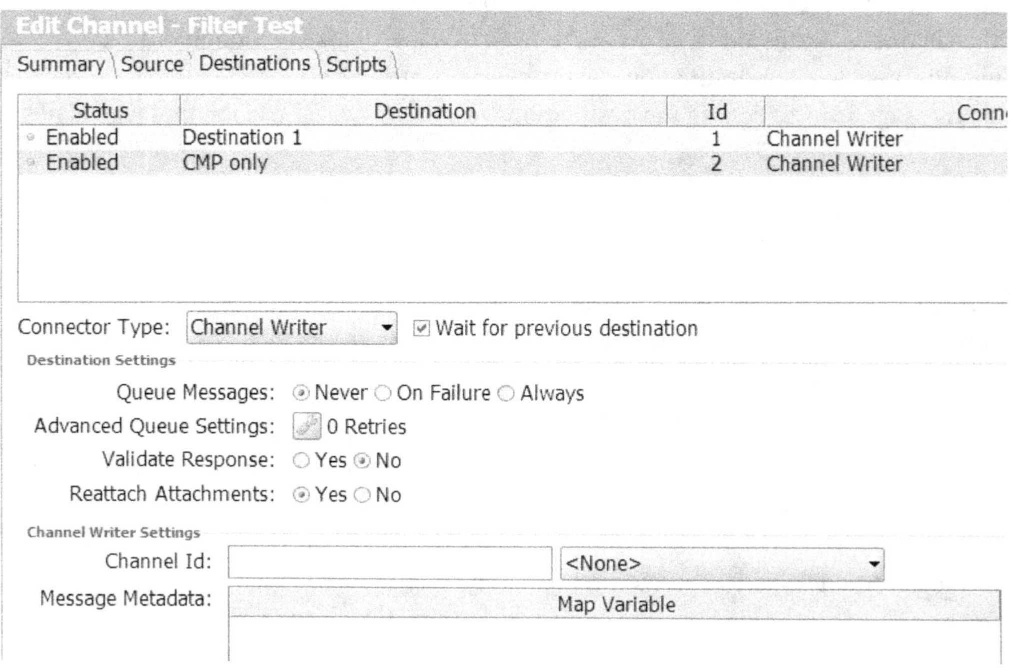

With the new destination's new name still highlighted, we can select Channel Tasks/Edit Filter on "Add Filter" which changes the main tab to an empty list of filters:

Edit Channel - Filter Test - CMP only Filter

Enabled	#	Name	Type

We select Filter Tasks/Add New Rule, and are given a new rule of type Rule Builder. We could stay with the rule builder interface, or switch to Javascript. Using the Rule Builder, we can enter the two sides of our comparison, entering the field we'd like to test in "Field:", the test requirement in "Condition:" and, clicking the "New" button to the right of the Values table, we can type in a new value: 'CMP'.

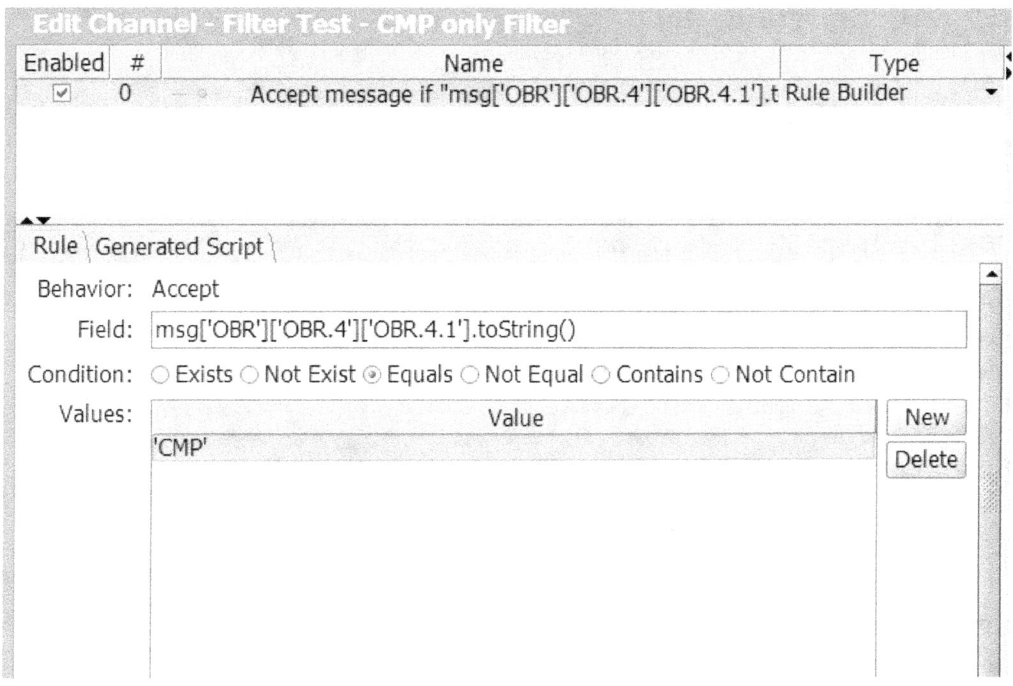

Mirth generates a script, which we can see by switching to the "Generated Script" tag. We could just as easily have right-clicked on "Rule Builder" in the right of our initial rule in the rule's listing, changed to Javascript, and typed in the script ourselves. We can add as many rules as we wish, linking them with AND or OR.

To test our rule, we go back to the channel, save it, deploy it, and send it a pair of test messages, one with the OBR.4.1 set to CMP and one without. When we deploy the channel, we are returned to the dashboard view, and if we highlight our new channel, we'll see "Send Message" as an option under Dashboard Tasks. Clicking it will give us a window into which we can type our message.

The first message we'll send is modified from an NIST sample. Because some segment lines print as more than one line, I've highlighted the segment names:

```
MSH|^~\&|^NISTLabs^L-CL^|^NIST^L-CL|^^|^^|20100407121000||
ORU^R01^ORU_R01|20100407121000|P|2.5.1|0001||AL||||MT-ORU-
2_R1
```

```
PID|1|9999|PT20^^^^AN||ZZLASTNAME^Jim^^^^^L||19500101|M|||
123 Testing Avenue^Apt. 999^ZZCITY^CA^90401||9998887777
ORC|RE|||ORD003-1^EHR-System
OBR|1|ORD003-1^EHR-System|LAB003^^NIST^L-CL|
CMP^Comprehensive Metabolic Panel^^^^|||20100407151000||||
L||||Arterial catheter|
000100^Butler^Internist^E^^Dr^MD^^^^^^EI||||RO||
20100407121000||CH|F
OBX|1|NM|13457-7^Fasting Blood Glucose^LN||178|mg/dl|70-
100 mg/dl|H|||F|||20100407121000||^DOE^JOHN|||||||Milton
Street Laboratory^^^^^CLIA^^^^10D987432|40025 Milton
Street^^Aurora^Colorado^80011|^Smith^John^^^Dr.^MD
OBX|2|NM|14682-9^Creatinine^LN||1.0|mg/dL|0.5-1.4||||
F|||||^DOE^JOHN|||||||Milton Street
Laboratory^^^^^CLIA^^^^10D987432|40025 Milton
Street^^Aurora^Colorado^80011|^Smith^John^^^Dr.^MD
OBX|3|NM|14647-2^BUN^LN||18|mg/dL|7-30||||F|||||
^DOE^JOHN|||||||Milton Street
Laboratory^^^^^CLIA^^^^10D987432|40025 Milton
Street^^Aurora^Colorado^80011|^Smith^John^^^Dr.^MD
SPM||||^Arterial catheter||||||||||||||||||||
HEM^Hemolyzed|
```

After sending it, we can examine the Dashboard statistics:

Dashboard — mirth connect

Status	Name	Rev Δ	Last Deplo...	Received	Filtered	Queued	Sent	Errored
Started	[Default Group]	--	--	0	0	0	2	0
Started	Filter Test	0	2020-09-0...	0	0	0	2	0
Started	Source	--	--	0	0	0	0	0
Started	Destination 1	--	--	1	0	0	1	0
Started	CMP only	--	--	1	0	0	1	0

We see that 1 message was received at the Source Transformer, one message was received at and sent by Destination 1, and one message was received at and sent by our new destination, CMP only. Let's send a different sample message:

```
MSH|^~\&|^NISTLabs^L-CL^|^NIST^L-CL|^^|^^|20100407121000||
ORU^R01^ORU_R01|20100407121000|P|2.5.1|0001||AL||||MT-ORU-
2_R1
PID|1|8888|PT21^^^^AN||ZZLASTNAME^ZZFIRST^^^^^L||19500101|
M|||123 Testing Avenue^Apt. 202^ZZCITY^CA^90401||
9998887777
ORC|RE|||ORD003-1^EHR-System
```

```
OBR|1|1^EHR-System|LAB003^^NIST^L-CL|087-0714^Electrolyte
panel^99Lab^80061^Electrolyte panel^C4|||
20100407151000||||L|||||
2^Robinson^William^E^^Dr^MD^^^^^^EI||||RO||
20100407121000||CH|F
OBX|1|NM|2951-2^Serum Sodium^LN||141|meq/l|135-146||||F|||
20100407121000||^DOE^JOHN|||||||Oakton Crest
Laboratories^^^^^CLIA^^^^10D987432|5570 Eden
Street^^Oakland^California^94607|^Smith^John^^^Dr.^MD
OBX|2|NM|2823-3^Serum Potassium^LN||4.3|meq/l|3.5-5.3||||
F|||20100407121000||^DOE^JOHN|||||||Oakton Crest
Laboratories^^^^^CLIA^^^^10D987432|5570 Eden
Street^^Oakland^California^94607|^Smith^John^^^Dr.^MD
```

The result with this message, which does not have CMP in its OBR.4.1, is that it is sent to the original destination but filtered -- not sent -- by our CMP_only destination:

Dashboard — mirth connect

Status	Name	Rev Δ	Last Deplo...	Received	Filtered	Queued	Sent	Errored
Started	[Default Group]	--	--	2	1	0	3	0
Started	Filter Test	0	2020-09-0...	2	1	0	3	0
Started	Source	--	--	2	0	0	0	0
Started	Destination 1	--	--	2	0	0	2	0
Started	CMP only	--	--	2	1	0	1	0

We can add a filter to the source connector as well, and if the source filter does not return true, the message does not get sent on to any destinations.

To avoid typing our field into the Rule Builder interface, we can add a message template to the Inbound Message Template, which will create a message tree with nodes we can drag to the "Field" area of our rule builder's rule:

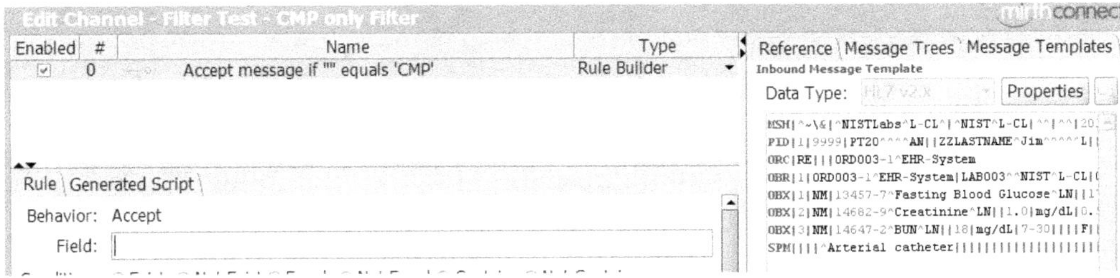

Switch from the Message Templates tab to the Message Trees tab to see the message expanded to tree form. Clicking on the boxed plus signs, expand a node path until you have the value of the OBR-4-1 node highlighted. Drag it across to the field area, and release it, and Mirth handles the typing and syntax for you.

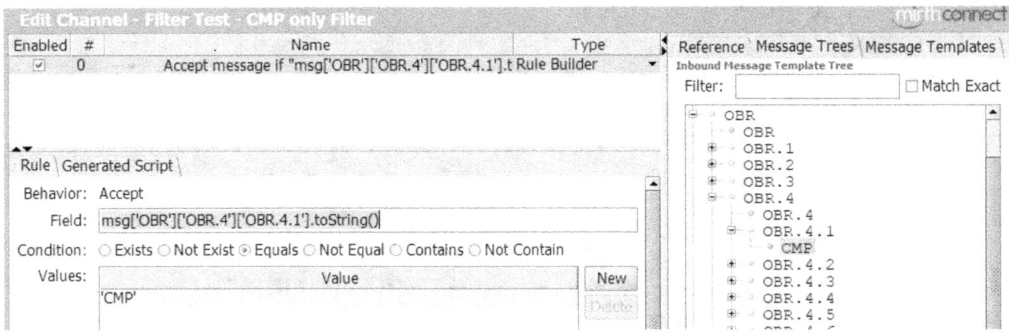

We can add filters to our source connector as well, which enables Mirth to entirely reject a message that does not fit what the channel expects.

Before we leave the subject of filtering, it's important to note that you may also directly remove destinations from the set of destination connectors to which the message will be forwarded by the source connector. In fact, Mirth provide a Java API to many of its objects, and clicking Other/View User API will bring up the API in a browser window.

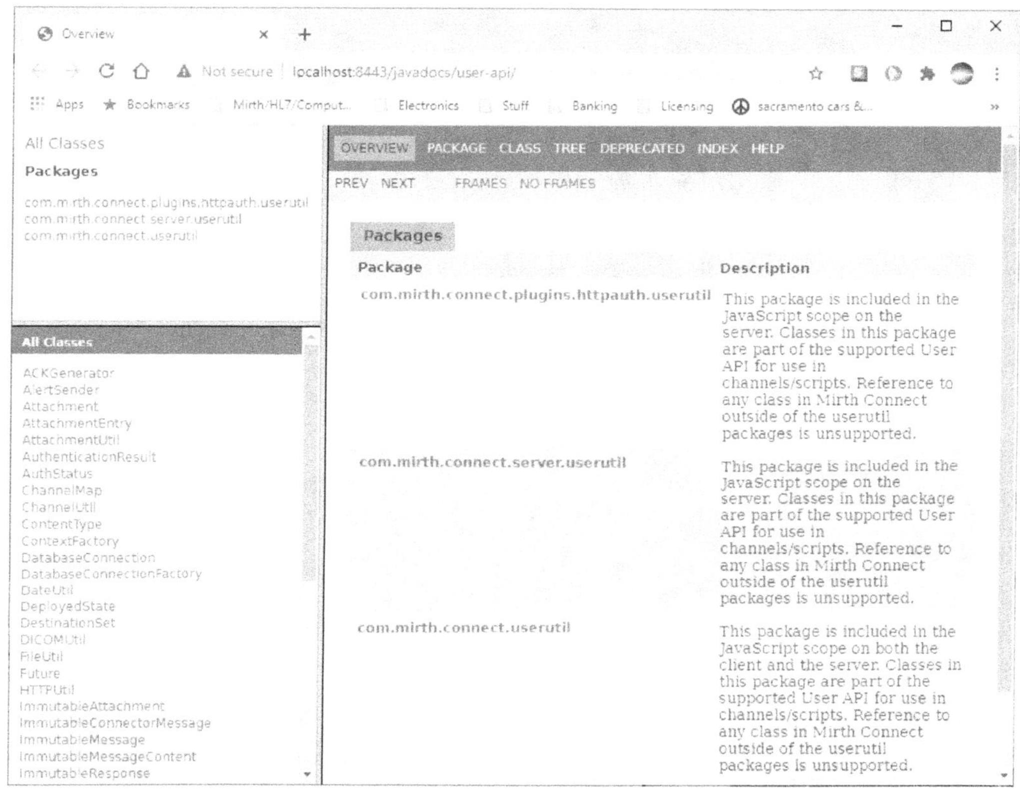

Lookingon the lower left of the screen, we find a class named DestinationSet, and we can click on it to bring up its documentation, which says you should not create instances of this class. That suggests that Mirth must create an instance, so how to get to it?

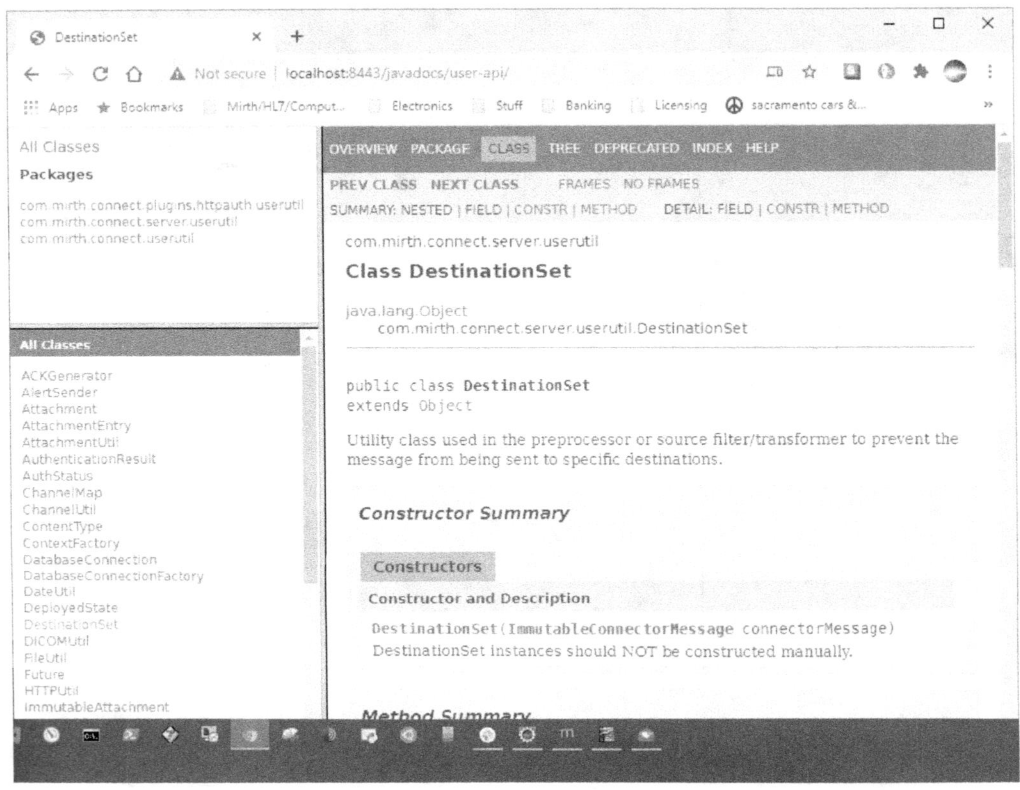

The answer lies in the "Reference" tab that comes up on the right hand side when you are working with Mirth transformers, along with the Message Template and Message Tree tabs. Clicking on Reference, we get a listing of various variable names and code fragments we can drag into a transformer; one is "Remove one or more from DestinationSet." Dragging it into the "Step" window of a Javascript transformer will add an appropriate one line code template to your Javascript.

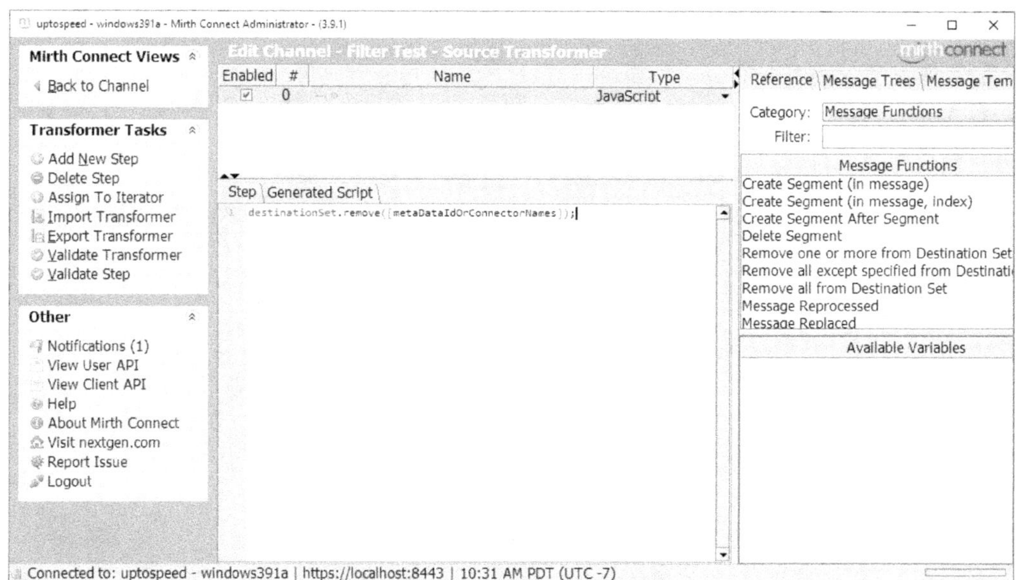

This would be a good time for you to stand up, take a breath and, when you come back to the computer, take a look at the various functions available. They're there to make your life easier.

Code Templates

As you begin creating more channels, you will probably find that many of the channels require the same message manipulation as others. You can store common routines in Mirth's Code Templates by creating one or more Code Template libraries and populating each with functions that can be called from your channels or code blocks that can be dragged into them.

When in channel view, select Channel Tasks/Edit Code Templates. Then select Code Template Tasks/New Library. An empty library will be created; you can rename it from the default value of Library1. Here we have renamed our new library to "Uptospeed" and indicated it should be available to all channels, including channels that we create later.

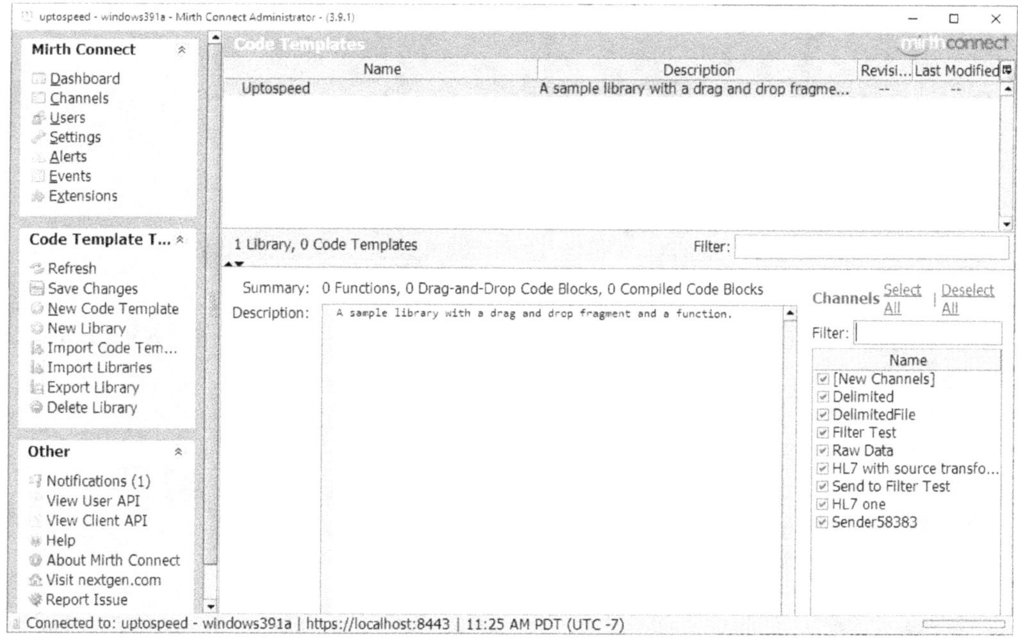

Now, we can add a few lines of code that we'd like to be able to copy into a channel's Javascript transformers.

We could, for example, provide code that copies the patient's last name into the channelMap, using the channelMap entry name "last_name."

Selecting Code Template Tasks/New Code Template, we see that Mirth proposes we write a Function, showing a function outline in an editing window.

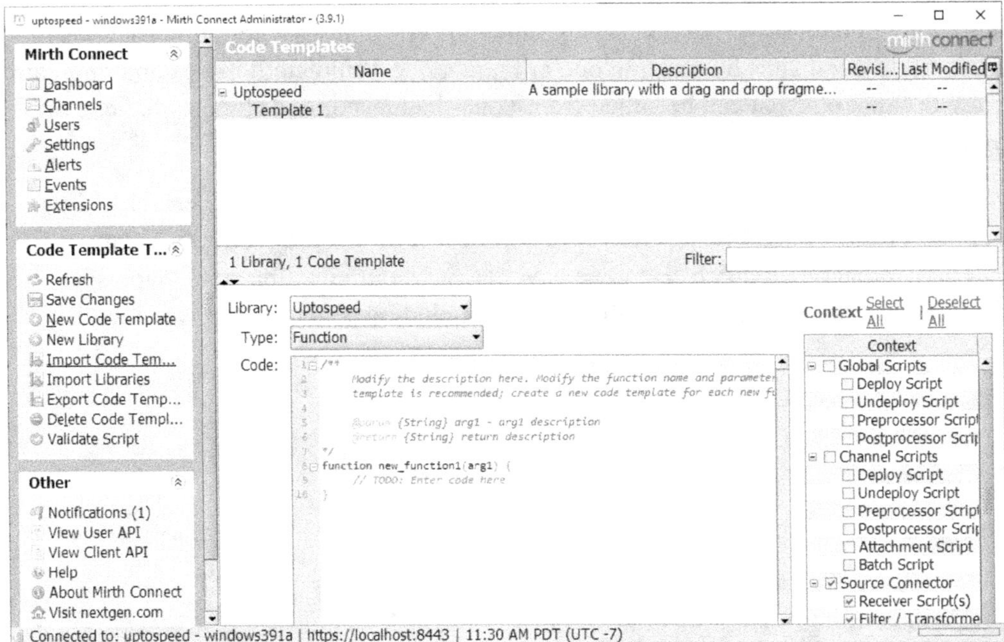

Let's change the Type from Function to Drag and Drop Code Block, rename it from Template1 to "Last_name to channelMap" and enter the code:

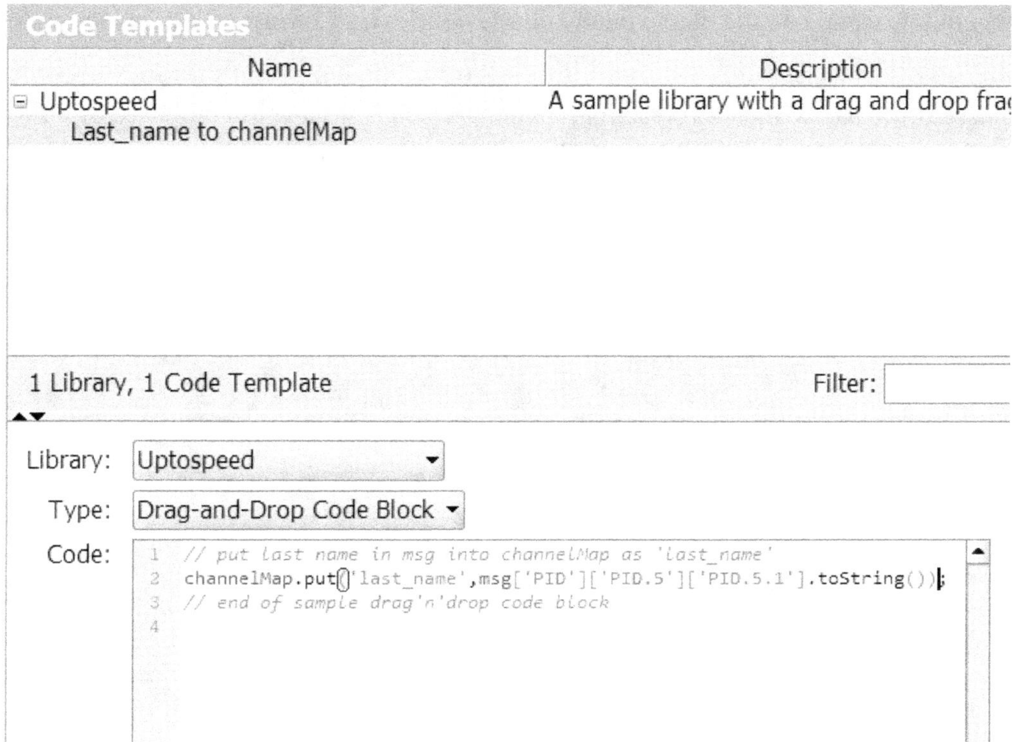

In the Reference tab, this code block now appears by name, in the category User Defined Code.

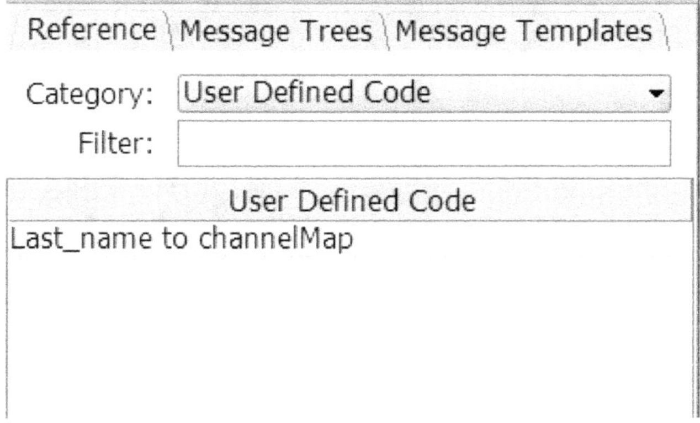

Dragging its name into the Step window of a Javascript transformer step drops the code in place.

If, instead, we had written a Javascript function (which is what Mirth proposed as a default), we would find the function in the Reference tab under the category User Defined Functions; dragging it into a Javascript transformer step will drop a call to the function. The argument list to the function will initially have your formal argument names; in this case, to use the function against my channel's msg variable, I need to change the formal argument name from hl7_msg to "msg." The function returns the PID-5-1 text from the message handed to it.

Instead of writing Javascript from within Mirth, we can define a transformer step type as "External Script." We are prompted for the filename of a Javascript file that the Mirth process will load each time the channel is deployed.

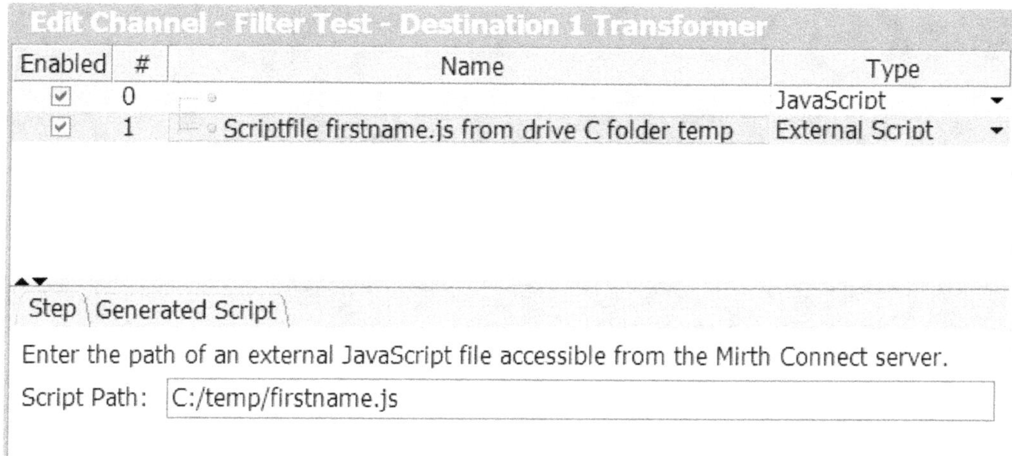

Note that the transformers are re-executed for every message that passes through the transformer's connector. If you would like to create a function once, such that it is available for use, rather than place its definition into a transformer, it would make sense to define it in your channel's deployment script and have that script load it into your channel's globalChannelMap. The function can then be retrieved by name from that map prior to use.

You have access to Java libraries from within transformers. Simply reference the appropriate package with the prefix Packages. For example, to reference Java's value for pi, from java.lang.Math, the line:

```
var jpi = Packages.java.lang.Math.PI
```

will work just fine.

Although writing custom Java code is beyond the scope of this small book, it's important to note that you can import your own Java JAR files into Mirth, and use your custom code from transformers if you wish.

Alerts and Responses

You'll probably want to be notified when something goes wrong. There are two mechanisms for this, the responses generated from message processing, and the alerting system.

To create an alert, select Alerts/New Alert. This will take you to a screen on which you can configure a new alert; name it in the name field and indicate which sort of error situation you'd like the alert to “fire” on.

If you will be manually invoking an alert from code, as opposed to alerting on an error recognized by Mirth, chcek “User Defined Transformer.” If you are interested in alerting on a particular error, you can check one or more processing phases which should trigger your alert.

Enable your alert, in the Channels area on the right, for all channels to which you'd like it to apply. Click on a channel and then click the Enable button, and the channel will turn from red to green. You can indicate that only certain connectors of a channel should be included, in which case the channel itself turns from red to yellow, while the enabled connector will turn green.

When the alert occurs, the actions you enter into the action list will occur. We'll ask that an email message be sent to an address. We can provide a subject line and message we'd like sent when the alert occurs, and can include information from the message by dragging it from the Alert Variables on the right into the template area.

Let's create a raw data channel named “Test Alert” with a Javascript transformer in its initial destination; we'll have the destination transformer use the built-in object named “alerts” to send an alert. We indicate the name of the alert we'd like to trigger, and include a message:

```
alerts.sendAlert('test_alert_1','here we are');
```

Now we have to create an alert named test_alert_1, enable it for “User Defined,” enable it on the channel “Test Alert,” and add an action to send email to an address, monitor@uptospeedbook.com.

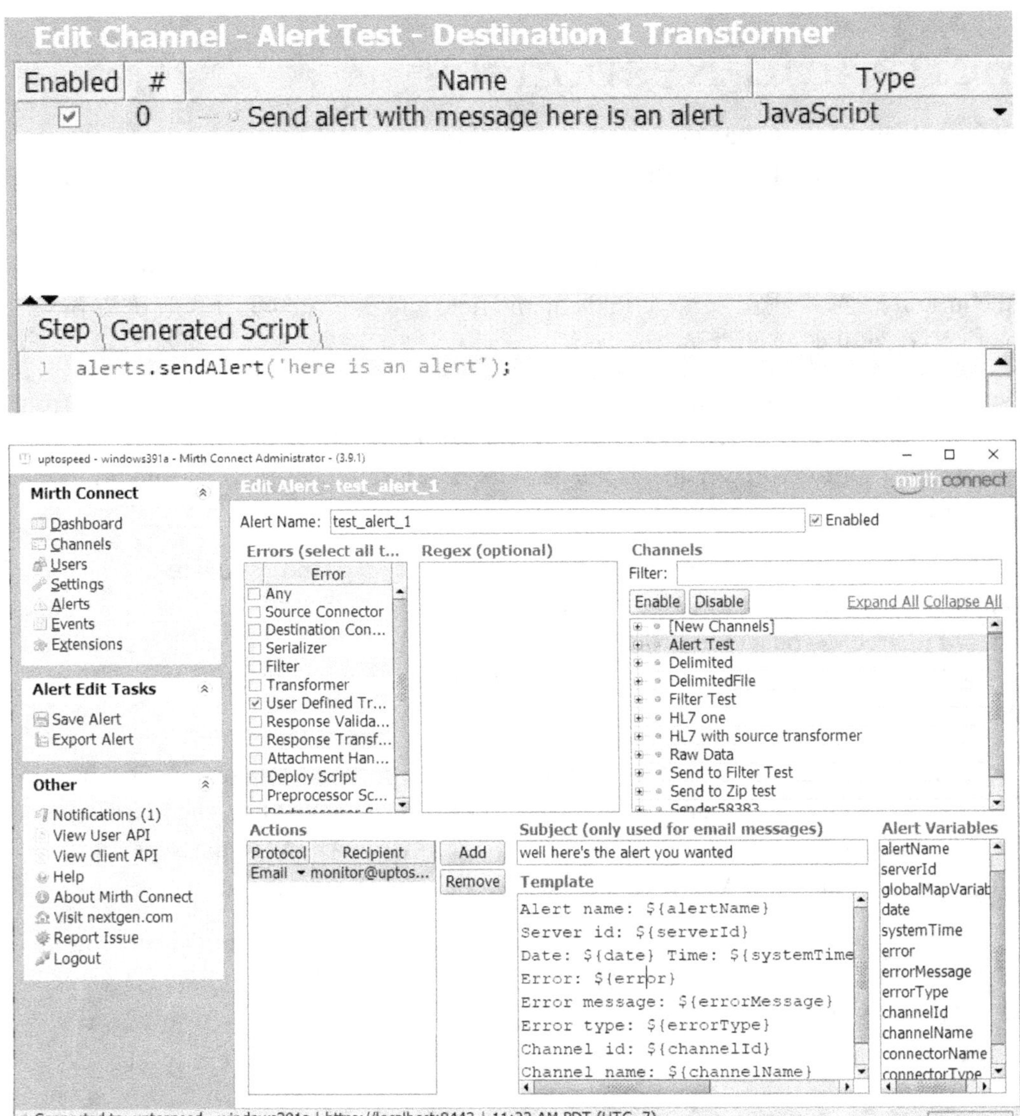

Let's send an HL7 message, any message will do, into this channel, so that we trigger the destination transformer. It will trigger the alert, which will send email:

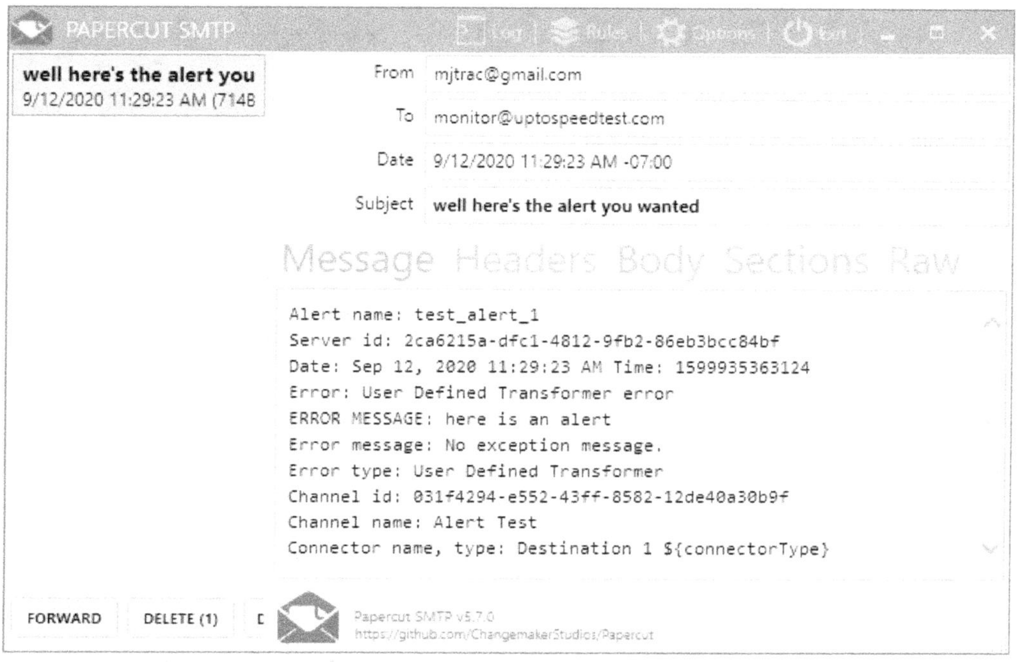

Let's edit our channel now, leaving the call to alerts.sendAlert and adding a line that will fail. For example, let's try assigning a nonexistent variable from the Java math library, PIE instead of PI, into our MSH-3-1 field:

msg['MSH']['MSH.3']['MSH.3.1'] = Packages.java.lang.math.PIE;

We'll add a second alert, but this time we'll set it to be triggered in any situation.

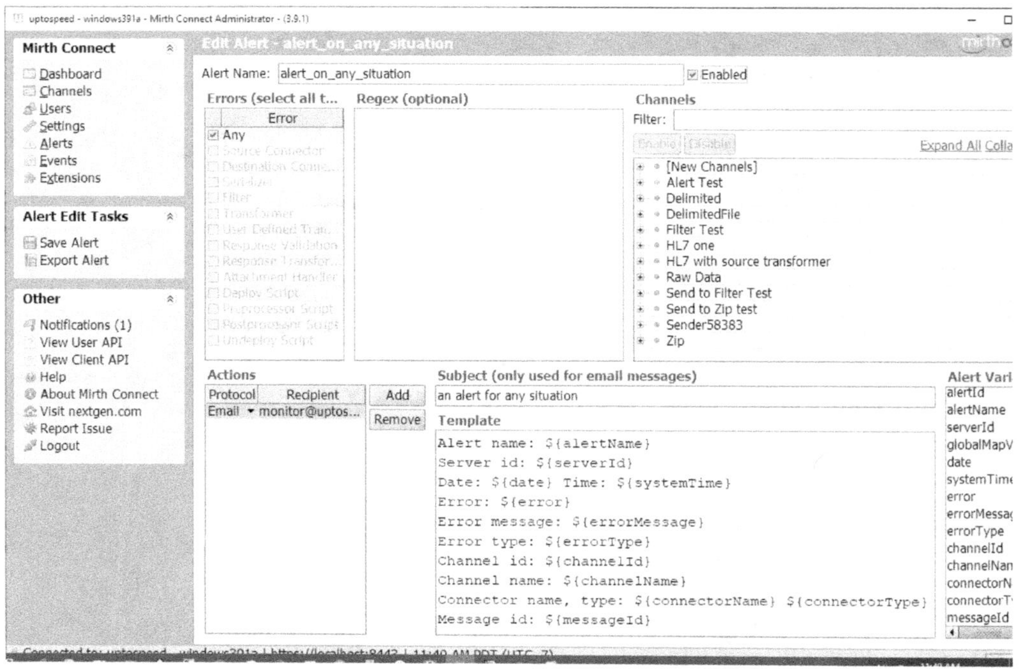

We can now redeploy our alerting channel and reprocess the message that has already been sent through it; we're going to get the alert from our alerts.sendAlert call, and then our second alert will fire twice – once as a result of the alerts.sendAlert call – remember, we did say Any for situation, and once for the transformer error. The latter email will look like this. Look closely and compare against our template, and you'll see that the stack trace is provided twice, once from ${error} and once from ${errorMessage}. I've bolded parts of the template in the material below, and italicized the most relevant part of the trace in order to make that more obvious. Also, notice that the time is included in the date variable, but in the time variable we are given the time as number of milliseconds into the "epoch," which began on New Year's Day in 1970 :

```
Alert name: alert_on_any_situation
Server id: 2ca6215a-dfc1-4812-9fb2-86eb3bcc84bf
Date: Sep 12, 2020 11:42:42 AM Time: 1599936162616
Error: Transformer error
ERROR MESSAGE: Error evaluating transformer
com.mirth.connect.server.MirthJavascriptTransformerException:
CHANNEL:         Alert Test
CONNECTOR:       Destination 1
SCRIPT SOURCE:   TRANSFORMER
```

```
SOURCE CODE:
103: if (msg.namespace('') != undefined) { default xml namespace =
msg.namespace(''); } else { default xml namespace = ''; }
104: function doFilter() { phase[0] = 'filter'; return true; }function
doTransform() { phase[0] = 'transformer'; logger =
Packages.org.apache.log4j.Logger.getLogger(phase[0]);
105:
106:
107: alerts.sendAlert('here is an alert');
108: msg['MSH']['MSH.3']['MSH.3.1'] = Packages.java.lang.Math.PIE;
109: if ('xml' === typeof msg) {
110:     if (msg.hasSimpleContent()) {
111:         msg = msg.toXMLString();
112:     }
LINE NUMBER:    108
DETAILS:        Java class "java.lang.Math" has no public instance field or method
named "PIE".
        at 1ce558f0-a9a4-48e8-9f18-7d9003e093bd:108 (doTransform)
        at 1ce558f0-a9a4-48e8-9f18-7d9003e093bd:130 (doScript)
        at 1ce558f0-a9a4-48e8-9f18-7d9003e093bd:132
        at
com.mirth.connect.server.transformers.JavaScriptFilterTransformer$FilterTransforme
rTask.doCall(JavaScriptFilterTransformer.java:154)
        at
com.mirth.connect.server.transformers.JavaScriptFilterTransformer$FilterTransforme
rTask.doCall(JavaScriptFilterTransformer.java:1)
        at
com.mirth.connect.server.util.javascript.JavaScriptTask.call(JavaScriptTask.java:1
13)
        at java.util.concurrent.FutureTask.run(Unknown Source)
        at java.util.concurrent.ThreadPoolExecutor.runWorker(Unknown Source)
        at java.util.concurrent.ThreadPoolExecutor$Worker.run(Unknown Source)
        at java.lang.Thread.run(Unknown Source)
```

Error message:

```
CHANNEL:        Alert Test
CONNECTOR:      Destination 1
SCRIPT SOURCE:  TRANSFORMER
SOURCE CODE:
103: if (msg.namespace('') != undefined) { default xml namespace =
msg.namespace(''); } else { default xml namespace = ''; }
104: function doFilter() { phase[0] = 'filter'; return true; }function
doTransform() { phase[0] = 'transformer'; logger =
Packages.org.apache.log4j.Logger.getLogger(phase[0]);
105:
106:
107: alerts.sendAlert('here is an alert');
108: msg['MSH']['MSH.3']['MSH.3.1'] = Packages.java.lang.Math.PIE;
109: if ('xml' === typeof msg) {
110:     if (msg.hasSimpleContent()) {
111:         msg = msg.toXMLString();
112:     }
```

```
LINE NUMBER:    108
DETAILS:        Java class "java.lang.Math" has no public instance field or method
named "PIE".
        at 1ce558f0-a9a4-48e8-9f18-7d9003e093bd:108 (doTransform)
        at 1ce558f0-a9a4-48e8-9f18-7d9003e093bd:130 (doScript)
        at 1ce558f0-a9a4-48e8-9f18-7d9003e093bd:132
Error type: Transformer
Channel id: 031f4294-e552-43ff-8582-12de40a30b9f
Channel name: Alert Test
Connector name, type: Destination 1 ${connectorType}
Message id: 1
```

This stack trace will also be visible when we look in the Dashboard at the message:

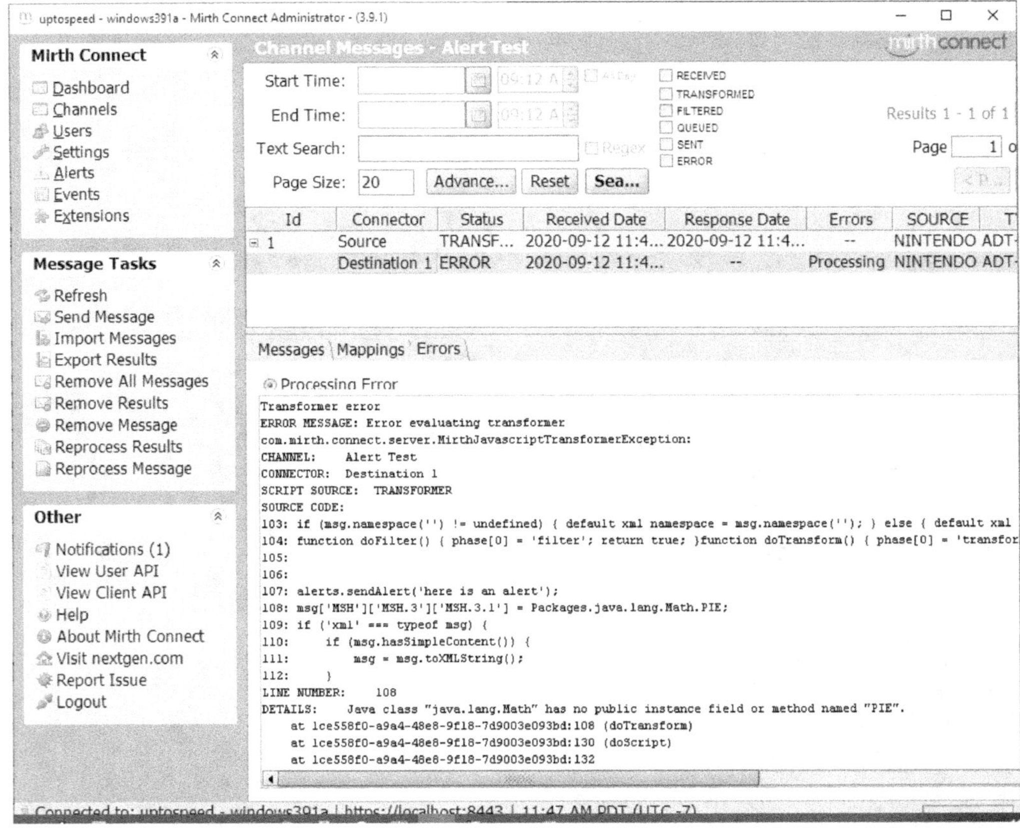

If you haven't seen that "Errors" tab when inspecting messages until now, congratulations, you've managed not to generate any errors yet!

When errors do occur in the processing of a message through a connector, you will have this errors tab available so that you can inspect the error that has occurred. In this case, we see that PIE is not a valid public field or method name in java.lang.Math. Note that your stack trace includes code that Mirth runs in order to run your transformer, in addition to the code you enter.

I've added an additional variable to the new alert's email – messageID. The ID that is provided is the same ID that will show in the channel's Dashboard for the message we've been working with, in this case, "1".

Responses

When Mirth receives a message, it by default automatically generates a response to the sending system. The response can be generated after different amounts of processing. Destination connectors also generate responses, and the source connector can also be configured to pass back the response from a particular destination.

In transmitting HL7, the sending system expects to receive a response HL7 message that includes an MSH message header segment and an MSA segment, whose second field will be set to the value AA if the message was accepted. As far back as HL7v2.1, the receiver could also send back an AE, indicating some error, or an AR, indicating the receiving system rejects the message.

For example, if a channel is expecting to receive a particular type of message, perhaps an ORU for lab results, it may choose to filter out an inbound ADT registration message sent by mistake. If it does this, it is expected to return an AR code in its acknowledgement. If the application instead tries to process the message but cannot validate it, it is expected to return an AE code. If the message is valid but there is some other reason the receiving system can't work with it, the receiving system is expected to send back an AR.

Starting with version 2.2, three additional possible codes were added, CA, CE, and CR, representing "commit accept," "commit error," and "commit reject." These are for use with messages that include MSH-15 and MSH-16 values, and can be used to indicate that the receiving application has successfully stored the incoming message.

Mirth will automatically generate a response for the sending system, and by default this takes place after source transformers (and filters). So if your message is filtered out at the source, Mirth will generate an AR acknowledgement, indicating that the message was rejected. If your message is accepted, it will send an AA, indicating that the message was accepted.

You can configure a channel to queue inbound messages for later processing; in that case, if you want to send a response, the response will have to be generated prior to the processing of the message.

To explore automatic and custom responses, we'll set up three channels:

- Send to Responder – sends to "Responder's" port on our local host
- Responder – retrieves messages, sends them to "From Responder's" port on localhost and sends responses to "Send to Responder"
- From Responder

This will enable us to see how messages pass through Responder.

In this example, Send to Responder will send, and Responder will listen on port 6662; Responder will send, and From Responder will listen on 6663.

Because these three channels form a natural grouping, let's create a new channel group, named Response Handling from the Channels view "Group Tasks" menu. Then, clicking on each of the channels in turn, we can select Group Tasks/Assign to Group to assign our three channels to Response Handling. In both Dashboard and Channel views, we can now focus in only on those three channels.

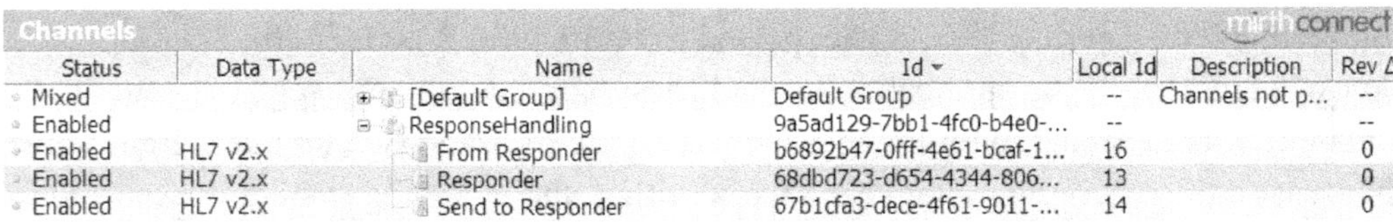

Channels

Status	Data Type	Name	Id	Local Id	Description	Rev Δ
Mixed		[Default Group]	Default Group	--	Channels not p...	--
Enabled		ResponseHandling	9a5ad129-7bb1-4fc0-b4e0-...	--		--
Enabled	HL7 v2.x	From Responder	b6892b47-0fff-4e61-bcaf-1...	16		0
Enabled	HL7 v2.x	Responder	68dbd723-d654-4344-806...	13		0
Enabled	HL7 v2.x	Send to Responder	67b1cfa3-dece-4f61-9011-...	14		0

Dashboard

Status	Name	Rev Δ	Last Deplo...	Received	Filtered	Queued	Sent
Started	ResponseHandling	--	--	0	0	0	0
Started	From Responder	0	2020-09-1...	0	0	0	0
Started	Send to Responder	0	2020-09-1...	0	0	0	0
Started	Responder	0	2020-09-1...	0	0	0	0
Mixed	[Default Group]	--	--	72	12	0	29

We've initially set Responder up to autogenerate a response after the source transformers have done any work:

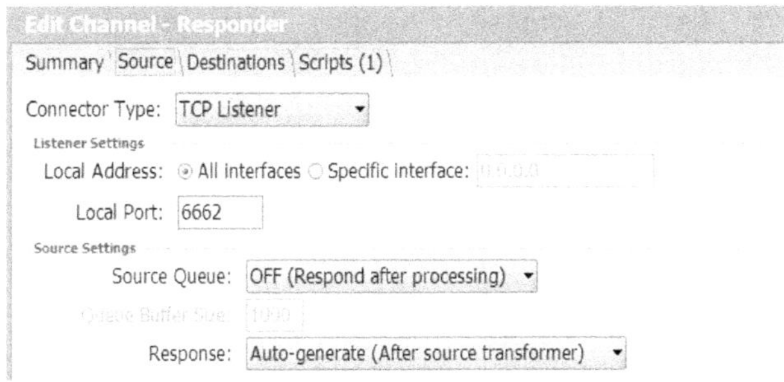

We'll take our standard sample message and send it from "Send to Responder," and look to see the response it receives. The dashboard view shows Send to Responder has sent one message; Responder received it and sent a copy to each of two destinations; From Responder (which shows one received) and a file writer destination.

Dashboard

Status	Name	Rev Δ	Last Deplo...	Received	Filtered	Queued	Sent
Started	From Responder	0	2020-09-1...	1	0	0	1
Started	Source	--	--	1	0	0	0
Started	Destination 1	--	--	1	0	0	1
Started	Send to Responder	0	2020-09-1...	1	0	0	1
Started	Source	--	--	1	0	0	0
Started	Send to port 6662	--	--	1	0	0	1
Started	Responder	0	2020-09-1...	1	0	0	2
Started	Source	--	--	1	0	0	0
Started	Send to 6663	--	--	1	0	0	1
Started	Write to file respond‹	--	--	1	0	0	1

We've added a Response Transformer to Send to Responder's Destination 1, which does nothing more than log its msg variable, so that it prints into our log file. But as a result of our having a Response Transformer, we have multiple views of the response received from Responder:

Messages | Mappings

○ Raw ○ Encoded ○ Sent ◉ Response ○ Response Transformed ○ Processed Response

Status:

```
SENT: Message successfully sent.
```

Response:

```
MSH|^~\&|TESTSYSTEM|TESTFACILITY|NES|NINTENDO|20200913105837.999||ACK|20200913105837.999|P|2.3
MSA|AA|Q123456789T123456789X123456
```

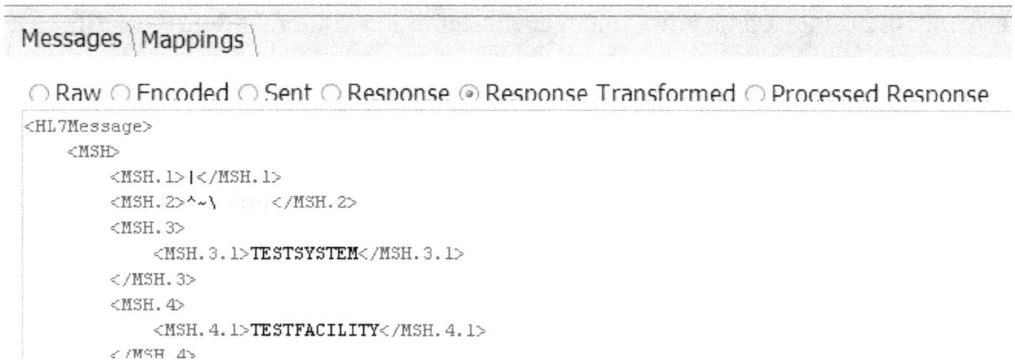

Messages | Mappings

○ Raw ○ Encoded ○ Sent ○ Response ⦿ Response Transformed ○ Processed Response

```
<HL7Message>
    <MSH>
        <MSH.1>|</MSH.1>
        <MSH.2>^~\ </MSH.2>
        <MSH.3>
            <MSH.3.1>TESTSYSTEM</MSH.3.1>
        </MSH.3>
        <MSH.4>
            <MSH.4.1>TESTFACILITY</MSH.4.1>
        </MSH.4>
```

Note that in the autogenerated response, the names of the sending and receiving systems and facilities in the MSH have been swapped from the way they were in the original message. Also, note that the original message control ID, from the MSH-10-1 of the original message, is presented in the MSA-2-1 of the response.

We can choose to pass back a response from any of our destinations, or from the postprocessor, by selecting them from the Response field of our source transformer.

Let's build an alternative response in the first of Responder's destinations. Select the appropriate Destination and then select Channel Tasks/Edit Response. Create a Javascript transformer. This time, the msg variable is for our response, so to see the original message, we had to put it, in text form, into our channelMap variable, and we retrieve it as the entry orig_msg:

Here's the code of our Response Transformer; we create our response as a string, substituting in fields from the original message, converted back to XML, and then register our response in Mirth's responseMap under the name "alternative". This name will then show in our source transformer's Response dropdown:

```
var orig = channelMap.get('original_msg');
var orig_as_xml = new XML(orig);
var msh3;
var msh4;
var msh9;
msh3 = orig_as_xml['MSH']['MSH.3']['MSH.3.1'].toString();
msh4 = orig_as_xml['MSH']['MSH.4']['MSH.4.1'].toString();
msh10 = orig_as_xml['MSH']['MSH.10']['MSH.10.1'].toString();
our_response = 'MSH|^~\&|OURAPP|OURFAC|';
our_response += msh3;
our_response += '|';
```

```
our_response += msh4;
our_response += '|';
var dateString = DateUtil.getCurrentDate('yyyyMMddHHmmss');
our_response += dateString;
// change inboung msg ctrl id to begin with, e.g., R in place of
pos 0
our_response += '||ACK|R'
our_response += msh10.substring(1);
our_response += '|P|2.3\r';
our_response += 'MSA|AA|'
our_response += msh10;
our_response += '|custom alternative message in MSA.3.1'
responseMap.put('alternative',
        ResponseFactory.getSentResponse(our_response)
);
```

In addition to our newly registered alternative response, we are offered the choice of the standard responses from our two named destinations, "Send to 6663" and "Write to file...", or a response from the Postprocessor.

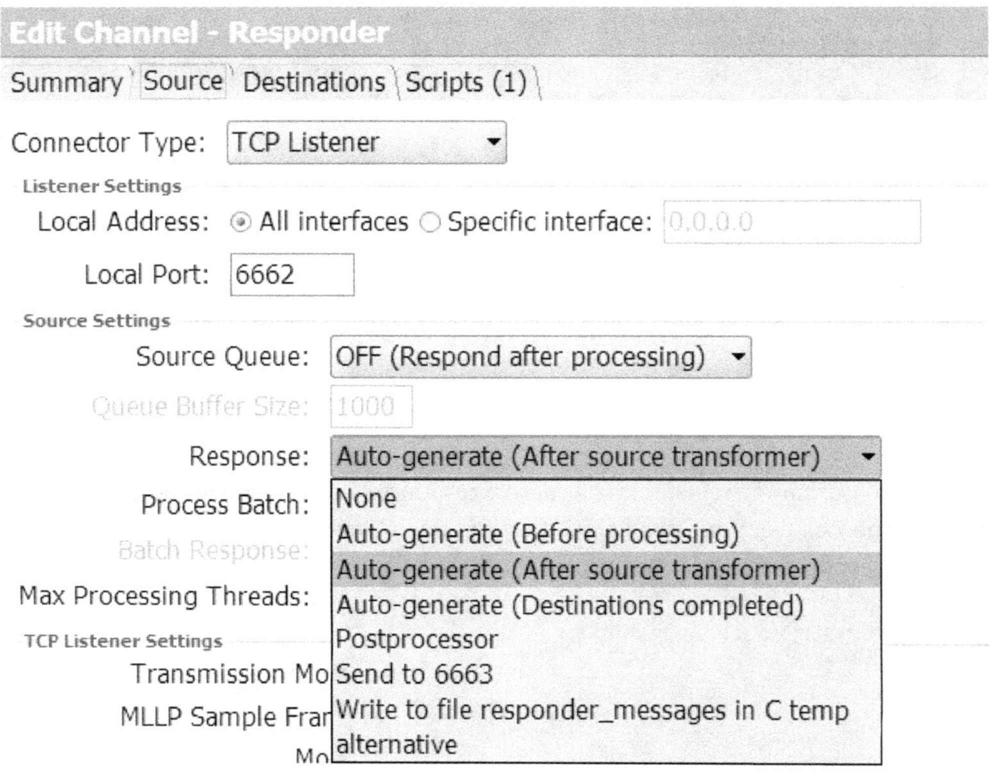

Let's save and redeploy Responder after switching to our alternative response, and send it our test message once again. This time, we get our assembled response, complete with a message written into MSA-3-1.

```
MSH|^~&|OURAPP|OURFAC|NES|NINTENDO|20200913112423||ACK|
    R123456789T123456789X123456|P|2.3
MSA|AA|Q123456789T123456789X123456|custom alternative message
    in MSA.3.1
```

Responses that a destination has generated are also available to subsequent destinations, as long as your destinations form a single, sequential chain, which is Mirth's default.

When highlighting the File Writer destination in Responder, which will not run until the TCPIP Writer destination Send to 6663 has completed, we can use "alternative" in our File Writer destination's template by dragging it from the Destination Mappings window on the right into our template, where it will appear as:

${alternative}. This ${} is a form of variable substitution provided by the Apache Java library named Velocity, and Velocity variables can be used in specifying values for many configuration fields of channels, not just for the message template.

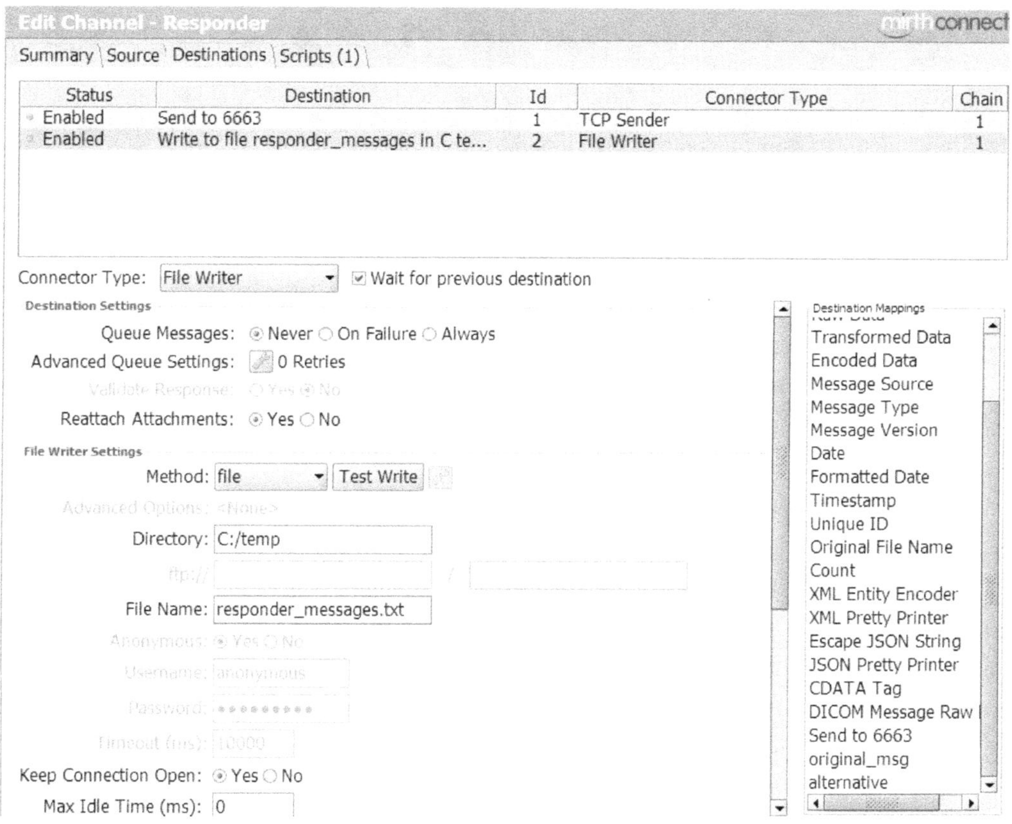

Sometimes, there's no need to wait for one destination to complete before running a second destination. In that case, you can simply uncheck the "Wait for previous destination checkbox while highlighting the independent destination in the Destinations tab:

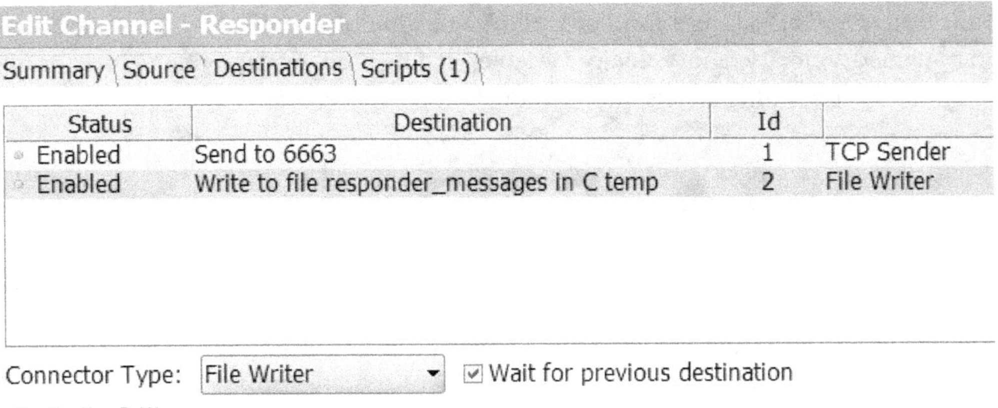

This will create a new "destination chain" starting with the selected destination. Destination chains can then operate in parallel rather than sequentially.

Building an HL7 message from Database Data

For some users, a common use case will be starting with a template HL7 message and filling in fields based on information from a lab system, spreadsheet, file, or database. This is one area where the Mirth user interface can assist with drag and drop capabilities.

We'll build a new database in Postgresql, with a table called Registrations, and we'll poll that table and generate ADT^A04 registration messages which are customized with the names. (You'd obviously want further customization, but we'll just demonstrate the technique here.)

We'll create a new channel whose source connector is a database reader, and whose source connector uses XML as its data type. The connector will perform database queries and offer up the results in XML. We'll set all data types to XML, except for the outbound data type of our destination, which will be HL7v2. Then, in our destination transformer, we'll enter an inbound template as XML and an outbound template built with HL7. First, from the Summary screen, we select Set Data Types and set XML:

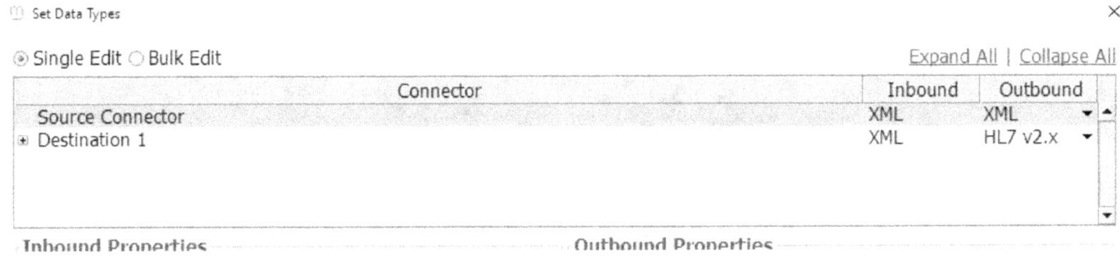

Then, we select a Database Reader for our source connector:

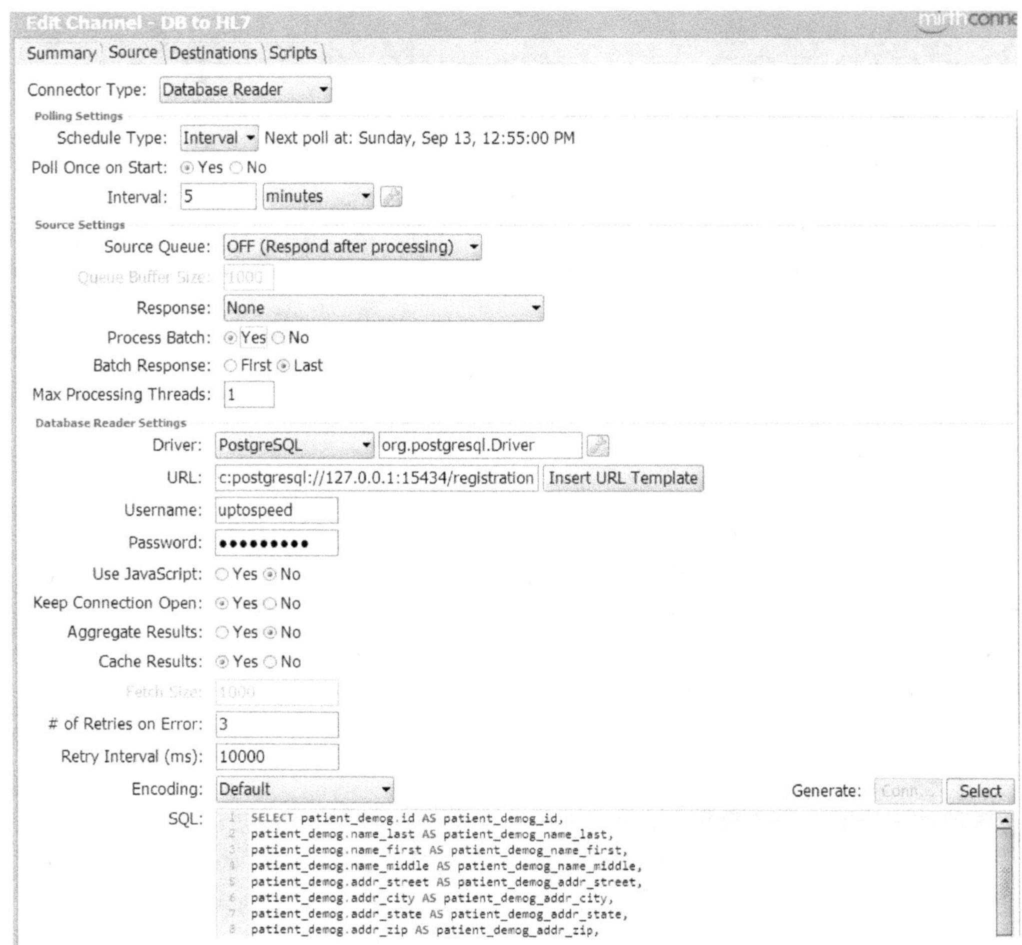

We've configured it to connect to a Postgresql database we've created, named registration. It is on a Postgresql server on our machine, communicating on port 15434, and the database is owned by user uptospeed. We will query this database every five minutes, and process in batch mode – each retrieved record will generate a new message. Mirth can build us a select statement when we click on the "Select" button at the extreme lower right of the screenshot above.

Assuming we have successfully configured things to connect with our database, clicking "Select" gets us a window with our database's tables and fields:

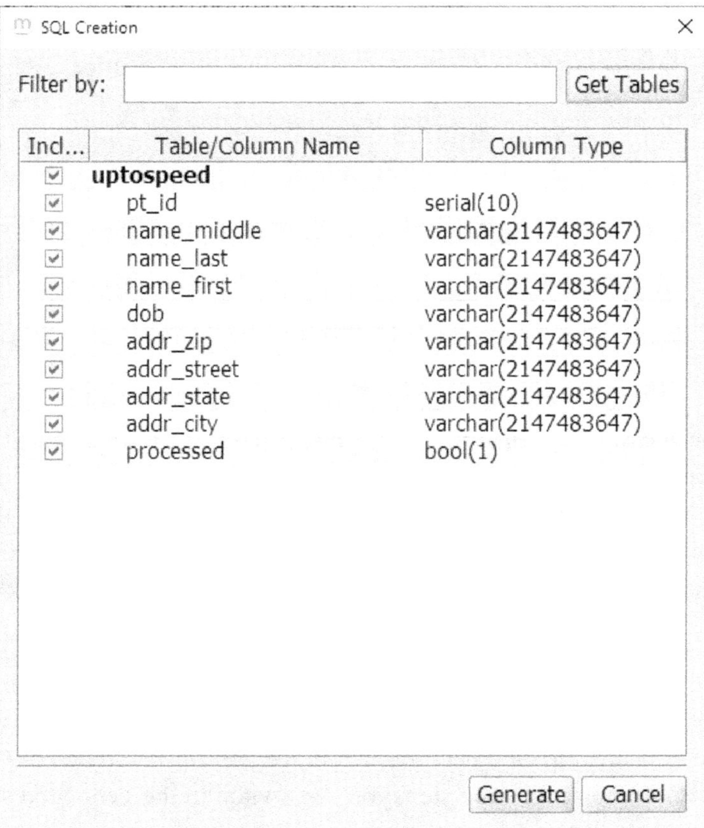

Selecting them all, we'll click generate, and the result will be the query that will be performed every five minutes. We'll want to modify it so that we only receive records that have not yet been processed. That just means adding "where not processed" to Mirth's automatically generated SQL.

Now it's time to go to our Destinations and set up our Destination 1 – we'll have it send to our Responder via TCPIP:

Our inbound template will look like this (we can run the channel once to pick up a message from the db in the correct format):

```
<result>
   <patient_demog_name_last>value</patient_demog_name_last>
   <patient_demog_name_first>value</patient_demog_name_first>
   <patient_demog_name_middle>value</patient_demog_name_middle>
   <patient_demog_addr_street>value</patient_demog_addr_street>
```

```
    <patient_demog_addr_city>value</patient_demog_addr_city>
    <patient_demog_addr_state>value</patient_demog_addr_state>
    <patient_demog_addr_zip>value</patient_demog_addr_zip>
    <patient_demog_processed>value</patient_demog_processed>
    <patient_demog_dob>value</patient_demog_dob>
</result>
```

Our outbound template will look like this:

```
MSH|^~\&|ADT1|MCM|LABADT|MCM|198808181126|SECURITY|ADT^A04|MSG00001|P|
2.4
EVN|A01-|198808181123
PID|||PATID1234^5^M11||JONES^WILLIAM^A||19610615|M-||2106-3|1200 N ELM
STREET^^GREENSBORO^NC^27401-1020|GL|(919)379-1212|(919)271-
3434~(919)277-3114||S||PATID12345001^2^M10|123456789|9-87654^NC
PV1|1|I|2000^2012^01||||004777^LEBAUER^SIDNEY^J.|||SUR||-||1|A0-
```

Switching to the Message Trees view, we get collapsed tree views of our incoming and outgoing templates. When we open paths and then drag the value shown in patient_demog_name_last down to JONES, which is the placeholder for Family Name in the outbound message template's PID segment, we are first prompted with whether we want to create an iterator. Let's say no; for more on iterators, you can look them up in the User Guide.

We repeat this drag and drop process with other fields, until we've instructed Mirth that its generated message should include the patient's last name, first name, given name, street address, city, state, zip, and date of birth in the appropriate fields of our outbound HL7 message. Remember, for each step, you can switch to the generated script tab to see what it would look like in Javascript; you just no longer need to worry about the awkward syntax.

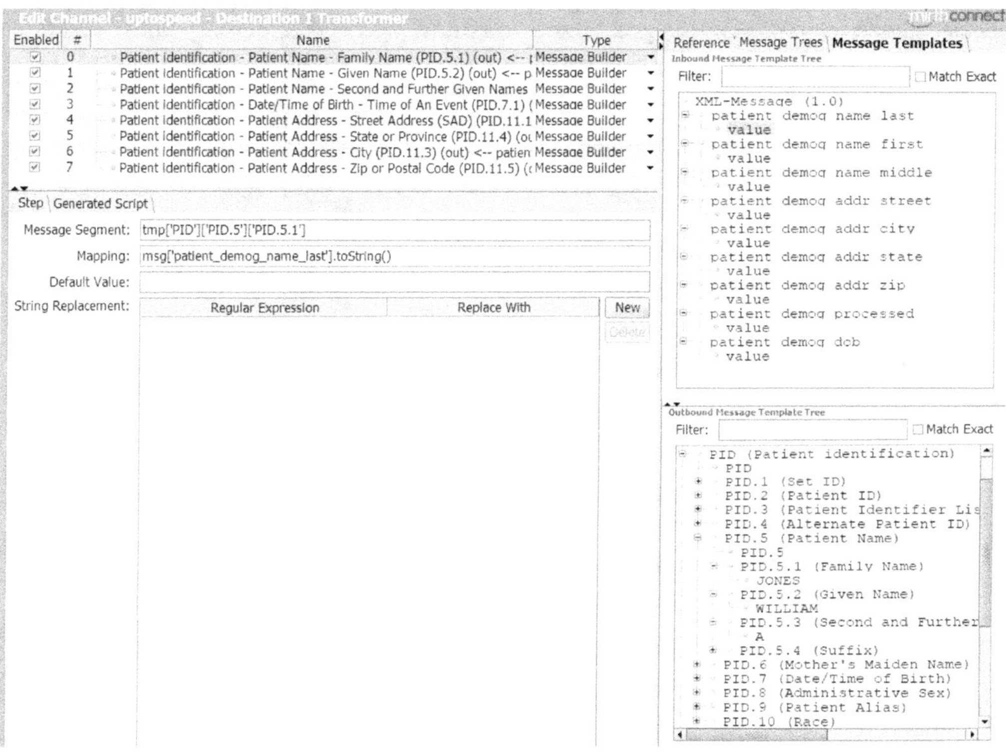

We are almost ready to deploy our channel, but it will keep pulling ALL the messages from our database. On the source connector, we need to put in an update SQL command to mark processed messages as processed.

Run Post-Process SQL: ○ Never ◉ After each message ○ Once after all messages

SQL:

```
update patient_demog set processed = True where id = ${patient_demog_id}
```

When we deploy, Mirth will now query the database at the interval specified, convert into XML each record that it retrieves, then substitutes that record's XML fields into the HL7 template we provided. Mirth will also update each processed record in the database, setting its processed field to True so that it is not picked up at the next interval.

This assistance from the GUI is great once you know what is happening, but if you don't understand what it is doing, you are very liable to get into trouble when you try to do anything out of the ordinary via Javascript. The User Guide goes into much more detail about the various drag-and-drop assistance, but I'll say it one last time; in my opinion, you should use the GUI assistance only once you understand the underlying code that it is generating. If you allow yourself to become dependent on it without knowing what it is doing, it's almost certain that you'll find yourself stumped by what is happening.

Congratulations! If you've made it this far, you're up to speed with Mirth Connect.

Epilogue

This book is not an exhaustive reference to Mirth Connect; it is intended to help new Mirth Connect users get up to speed on the fundamental capabilities present, and to make sense of some of the syntax involved in writing Javascript code that accesses HL7.

There is plenty more to learn; Mirth is like a multitool, and we've only explored some of the main tools. There are other connector types for specialized data types and transport protocols. You'll want to look at the Data Pruner to keep your Mirth database from becoming too large; it grows rapidly due to the number of copies of each message that will be stored.

You'll want to look at the configuration map, which is filled when Mirth starts with configuration variables pulled from a file in Mirth's configuration directory. Using this configuration data, you can have one Mirth instance serve as a test environment and another serve as a production environment, with the same code accessing different databases because their databases can be pulled from the configurationMap into your channels.

You'll want to look into the Mirth command line tool, and especially the API which has been made available and enhanced in recent versions, and can replace the Administrator in many situations.

I hope this brief book was of value to you. If you have comments or would like to make suggestions for improvements or tell me about any errors, please email me at mjtrac+mirth@gmail.com. Errors will be noted at my website, mitchtrachtenberg.com, and I provide exported versions of the book's channels.

Thanks for reading.

Appendices

Appendix A – An Exported Message

The following XML is what is captured when a simple message is exported as serialized XML; as you can see, multiple versions are captured:


```
<message>
 <messageId>1</messageId>
 <serverId>2ca6215a-dfc1-4812-9fb2-86eb3bcc84bf</serverId>
 <channelId>dfce4568-9686-47eb-992e-883eebbbf21c</channelId>
 <receivedDate>
 <time>1599494308066</time>
 <timezone>America/Los_Angeles</timezone>
 </receivedDate>
 <processed>true</processed>
 <connectorMessages class="linked-hash-map">
 <entry>
 <int>0</int>
 <connectorMessage>
 <messageId>1</messageId>
 <metaDataId>0</metaDataId>
 <channelId>dfce4568-9686-47eb-992e-883eebbbf21c</channelId>
 <channelName>Delimited</channelName>
 <connectorName>Source</connectorName>
 <serverId>2ca6215a-dfc1-4812-9fb2-86eb3bcc84bf</serverId>
 <receivedDate>
 <time>1599494308066</time>
 <timezone>America/Los_Angeles</timezone>
 </receivedDate>
 <status>TRANSFORMED</status>
 <raw>
 <encrypted>false</encrypted>
 <channelId>dfce4568-9686-47eb-992e-883eebbbf21c</channelId>
 <messageId>1</messageId>
 <metaDataId>0</metaDataId>
 <contentType>RAW</contentType>
 <content>Hello, Mirth!</content>
 <dataType>DELIMITED</dataType>
 </raw>
 <transformed>
 <encrypted>false</encrypted>
 <channelId>dfce4568-9686-47eb-992e-883eebbbf21c</channelId>
 <messageId>1</messageId>
 <metaDataId>0</metaDataId>
 <contentType>TRANSFORMED</contentType>
```

```
<content>&lt;delimited&gt;&lt;row&gt;&lt;column1&gt;Hello&lt;/column1&gt;&lt;colum
n2&gt; Mirth!&lt;/column2&gt;&lt;/row&gt;&lt;/delimited&gt;</content>
          <dataType>XML</dataType>
        </transformed>
        <encoded>
          <encrypted>false</encrypted>
          <channelId>dfce4568-9686-47eb-992e-883eebbbf21c</channelId>
          <messageId>1</messageId>
          <metaDataId>0</metaDataId>
          <contentType>ENCODED</contentType>
          <content>Hello, Mirth!
</content>
          <dataType>DELIMITED</dataType>
        </encoded>
        <sourceMapContent>
          <encrypted>false</encrypted>
          <content class="java.util.Collections$UnmodifiableMap">
            <m>
              <entry>
                <string>destinationSet</string>
                <linked-hash-set>
                  <int>1</int>
                </linked-hash-set>
              </entry>
            </m>
          </content>
        </sourceMapContent>
        <connectorMapContent>
          <encrypted>false</encrypted>
          <content class="map"/>
        </connectorMapContent>
        <channelMapContent>
          <encrypted>false</encrypted>
          <content class="map">
            <entry>
              <string>first_column</string>
              <string>Hello</string>
            </entry>
          </content>
        </channelMapContent>
        <responseMapContent>
          <encrypted>false</encrypted>
          <content class="map">
            <entry>
              <string>d1</string>
              <response>
                <status>SENT</status>
                <message></message>
                <statusMessage>Message routed successfully to channel id:
none</statusMessage>
              </response>
```

```
          </entry>
        </content>
      </responseMapContent>
      <metaDataMap/>
      <processingErrorContent>
        <encrypted>false</encrypted>
      </processingErrorContent>
      <postProcessorErrorContent>
        <encrypted>false</encrypted>
      </postProcessorErrorContent>
      <responseErrorContent>
        <encrypted>false</encrypted>
      </responseErrorContent>
      <errorCode>0</errorCode>
      <sendAttempts>1</sendAttempts>
      <responseDate>
        <time>1599494308100</time>
        <timezone>America/Los_Angeles</timezone>
      </responseDate>
      <chainId>0</chainId>
      <orderId>0</orderId>
    </connectorMessage>
  </entry>
  <entry>
    <int>1</int>
    <connectorMessage>
      <messageId>1</messageId>
      <metaDataId>1</metaDataId>
      <channelId>dfce4568-9686-47eb-992e-883eebbbf21c</channelId>
      <channelName>Delimited</channelName>
      <connectorName>Destination 1</connectorName>
      <serverId>2ca6215a-dfc1-4812-9fb2-86eb3bcc84bf</serverId>
      <receivedDate>
        <time>1599494308079</time>
        <timezone>America/Los_Angeles</timezone>
      </receivedDate>
      <status>SENT</status>
      <raw>
        <encrypted>false</encrypted>
        <channelId>dfce4568-9686-47eb-992e-883eebbbf21c</channelId>
        <messageId>1</messageId>
        <metaDataId>1</metaDataId>
        <contentType>RAW</contentType>
        <content>Hello, Mirth!
</content>
        <dataType>DELIMITED</dataType>
      </raw>
      <transformed>
        <encrypted>false</encrypted>
        <channelId>dfce4568-9686-47eb-992e-883eebbbf21c</channelId>
        <messageId>1</messageId>
```

```
          <metaDataId>1</metaDataId>
          <contentType>TRANSFORMED</contentType>

<content>&lt;delimited&gt;&lt;row&gt;&lt;column1&gt;Hello&lt;/column1&gt;&lt;colum
n2&gt; Mirth!&lt;/column2&gt;&lt;/row&gt;&lt;/delimited&gt;</content>
          <dataType>XML</dataType>
        </transformed>
        <encoded>
          <encrypted>false</encrypted>
          <channelId>dfce4568-9686-47eb-992e-883eebbbf21c</channelId>
          <messageId>1</messageId>
          <metaDataId>1</metaDataId>
          <contentType>ENCODED</contentType>
          <content>Hello, Mirth!
</content>
          <dataType>DELIMITED</dataType>
        </encoded>
        <sent>
          <encrypted>false</encrypted>
          <channelId>dfce4568-9686-47eb-992e-883eebbbf21c</channelId>
          <messageId>1</messageId>
          <metaDataId>1</metaDataId>
          <contentType>SENT</contentType>
          <content>&lt;com.mirth.connect.connectors.vm.VmDispatcherProperties
version=&quot;3.9.1&quot;&gt;
  &lt;pluginProperties/&gt;
  &lt;destinationConnectorProperties version=&quot;3.9.1&quot;&gt;
    &lt;queueEnabled&gt;false&lt;/queueEnabled&gt;
    &lt;sendFirst&gt;false&lt;/sendFirst&gt;
    &lt;retryIntervalMillis&gt;10000&lt;/retryIntervalMillis&gt;
    &lt;regenerateTemplate&gt;false&lt;/regenerateTemplate&gt;
    &lt;retryCount&gt;0&lt;/retryCount&gt;
    &lt;rotate&gt;false&lt;/rotate&gt;
    &lt;includeFilterTransformer&gt;false&lt;/includeFilterTransformer&gt;
    &lt;threadCount&gt;1&lt;/threadCount&gt;
    &lt;threadAssignmentVariable&gt;&lt;/threadAssignmentVariable&gt;
    &lt;validateResponse&gt;false&lt;/validateResponse&gt;
    &lt;resourceIds class=&quot;linked-hash-map&quot;&gt;
      &lt;entry&gt;
        &lt;string&gt;Default Resource&lt;/string&gt;
        &lt;string&gt;[Default Resource]&lt;/string&gt;
      &lt;/entry&gt;
    &lt;/resourceIds&gt;
    &lt;queueBufferSize&gt;1000&lt;/queueBufferSize&gt;
    &lt;reattachAttachments&gt;true&lt;/reattachAttachments&gt;
  &lt;/destinationConnectorProperties&gt;
  &lt;channelId&gt;none&lt;/channelId&gt;
  &lt;channelTemplate&gt;First column had: $c(&amp;apos;first_column&amp;apos;)

First column dragged in had: Hello&lt;/channelTemplate&gt;
```

```
  &lt;mapVariables/&gt;
&lt;/com.mirth.connect.connectors.vm.VmDispatcherProperties&gt;</content>
        </sent>
        <response>
          <encrypted>false</encrypted>
          <channelId>dfce4568-9686-47eb-992e-883eebbbf21c</channelId>
          <messageId>1</messageId>
          <metaDataId>1</metaDataId>
          <contentType>RESPONSE</contentType>
          <content>&lt;response&gt;
  &lt;status&gt;SENT&lt;/status&gt;
  &lt;message&gt;&lt;/message&gt;
  &lt;statusMessage&gt;Message routed successfully to channel id:
none&lt;/statusMessage&gt;
&lt;/response&gt;</content>
          <dataType>DELIMITED</dataType>
        </response>
        <sourceMapContent>
          <encrypted>false</encrypted>
          <content class="java.util.Collections$UnmodifiableMap">
            <m>
              <entry>
                <string>destinationSet</string>
                <linked-hash-set>
                  <int>1</int>
                </linked-hash-set>
              </entry>
            </m>
          </content>
        </sourceMapContent>
        <connectorMapContent>
          <encrypted>false</encrypted>
          <content class="map"/>
        </connectorMapContent>
        <channelMapContent>
          <encrypted>false</encrypted>
          <content class="map">
            <entry>
              <string>x</string>
              <string>x </string>
            </entry>
            <entry>
              <string>first_column</string>
              <string>Hello</string>
            </entry>
          </content>
        </channelMapContent>
        <responseMapContent>
          <encrypted>false</encrypted>
          <content class="map">
            <entry>
```

```
            &lt;string&gt;d1&lt;/string&gt;
            &lt;response&gt;
              &lt;status&gt;SENT&lt;/status&gt;
              &lt;message&gt;&lt;/message&gt;
              &lt;statusMessage&gt;Message routed successfully to channel id:
none&lt;/statusMessage&gt;
            &lt;/response&gt;
          &lt;/entry&gt;
        &lt;/content&gt;
      &lt;/responseMapContent&gt;
      &lt;metaDataMap/&gt;
      &lt;processingErrorContent&gt;
        &lt;encrypted&gt;false&lt;/encrypted&gt;
      &lt;/processingErrorContent&gt;
      &lt;postProcessorErrorContent&gt;
        &lt;encrypted&gt;false&lt;/encrypted&gt;
      &lt;/postProcessorErrorContent&gt;
      &lt;responseErrorContent&gt;
        &lt;encrypted&gt;false&lt;/encrypted&gt;
      &lt;/responseErrorContent&gt;
      &lt;errorCode&gt;0&lt;/errorCode&gt;
      &lt;sendAttempts&gt;1&lt;/sendAttempts&gt;
      &lt;sendDate&gt;
        &lt;time&gt;1599494308095&lt;/time&gt;
        &lt;timezone&gt;America/Los_Angeles&lt;/timezone&gt;
      &lt;/sendDate&gt;
      &lt;responseDate&gt;
        &lt;time&gt;1599494308095&lt;/time&gt;
        &lt;timezone&gt;America/Los_Angeles&lt;/timezone&gt;
      &lt;/responseDate&gt;
      &lt;chainId&gt;1&lt;/chainId&gt;

    &lt;orderId&gt;1&lt;/orderId&gt;
     &lt;/connectorMessage&gt;
    &lt;/entry&gt;
  &lt;/connectorMessages&gt;
&lt;/message&gt;
```

Appendix B – An Exported Raw Channel


```
<channel version="3.9.1">
  <id>b7825f33-27a7-4cbb-958c-82c703001af5</id>
  <nextMetaDataId>2</nextMetaDataId>
  <name>Raw Data</name>
  <description>A sample channel to see how Mirth handles raw data. </description>
  <revision>5</revision>
  <sourceConnector version="3.9.1">
    <metaDataId>0</metaDataId>
    <name>sourceConnector</name>
    <properties class="com.mirth.connect.connectors.vm.VmReceiverProperties" version="3.9.1">
      <pluginProperties/>
      <sourceConnectorProperties version="3.9.1">
        <responseVariable>None</responseVariable>
        <respondAfterProcessing>true</respondAfterProcessing>
        <processBatch>false</processBatch>
        <firstResponse>false</firstResponse>
        <processingThreads>1</processingThreads>
        <resourceIds class="linked-hash-map">
          <entry>
            <string>Default Resource</string>
            <string>[Default Resource]</string>
          </entry>
        </resourceIds>
        <queueBufferSize>1000</queueBufferSize>
      </sourceConnectorProperties>
    </properties>
    <transformer version="3.9.1">
      <elements>
        <com.mirth.connect.plugins.javascriptstep.JavaScriptStep version="3.9.1">
          <name>Dummy</name>
          <sequenceNumber>0</sequenceNumber>
          <enabled>true</enabled>
          <script>// do nothing</script>
        </com.mirth.connect.plugins.javascriptstep.JavaScriptStep>
      </elements>
      <inboundTemplate encoding="base64"></inboundTemplate>
      <outboundTemplate encoding="base64"></outboundTemplate>
      <inboundDataType>RAW</inboundDataType>
      <outboundDataType>RAW</outboundDataType>
      <inboundProperties class="com.mirth.connect.plugins.datatypes.raw.RawDataTypeProperties"
version="3.9.1">
        <batchProperties class="com.mirth.connect.plugins.datatypes.raw.RawBatchProperties"
version="3.9.1">
          <splitType>JavaScript</splitType>
          <batchScript></batchScript>
        </batchProperties>
      </inboundProperties>
      <outboundProperties
class="com.mirth.connect.plugins.datatypes.raw.RawDataTypeProperties" version="3.9.1">
        <batchProperties class="com.mirth.connect.plugins.datatypes.raw.RawBatchProperties"
version="3.9.1">
          <splitType>JavaScript</splitType>
          <batchScript></batchScript>
```

```
        </batchProperties>
      </outboundProperties>
    </transformer>
    <filter version="3.9.1">
      <elements/>
    </filter>
    <transportName>Channel Reader</transportName>
    <mode>SOURCE</mode>
    <enabled>true</enabled>
    <waitForPrevious>true</waitForPrevious>
  </sourceConnector>
  <destinationConnectors>
    <connector version="3.9.1">
      <metaDataId>1</metaDataId>
      <name>Destination 1</name>
      <properties class="com.mirth.connect.connectors.vm.VmDispatcherProperties"
version="3.9.1">
        <pluginProperties/>
        <destinationConnectorProperties version="3.9.1">
          <queueEnabled>false</queueEnabled>
          <sendFirst>false</sendFirst>
          <retryIntervalMillis>10000</retryIntervalMillis>
          <regenerateTemplate>false</regenerateTemplate>
          <retryCount>0</retryCount>
          <rotate>false</rotate>
          <includeFilterTransformer>false</includeFilterTransformer>
          <threadCount>1</threadCount>
          <threadAssignmentVariable></threadAssignmentVariable>
          <validateResponse>false</validateResponse>
          <resourceIds class="linked-hash-map">
            <entry>
              <string>Default Resource</string>
              <string>[Default Resource]</string>
            </entry>
          </resourceIds>
          <queueBufferSize>1000</queueBufferSize>
          <reattachAttachments>true</reattachAttachments>
        </destinationConnectorProperties>
        <channelId>none</channelId>
        <channelTemplate>${message.encodedData}</channelTemplate>
        <mapVariables/>
      </properties>
      <transformer version="3.9.1">
        <elements>
          <com.mirth.connect.plugins.javascriptstep.JavaScriptStep version="3.9.1">
            <name>Dummy</name>
            <sequenceNumber>0</sequenceNumber>
            <enabled>true</enabled>
            <script>// do nothing</script>
          </com.mirth.connect.plugins.javascriptstep.JavaScriptStep>
        </elements>
        <inboundTemplate encoding="base64"></inboundTemplate>
        <outboundTemplate encoding="base64"></outboundTemplate>
        <inboundDataType>RAW</inboundDataType>
        <outboundDataType>RAW</outboundDataType>
        <inboundProperties
class="com.mirth.connect.plugins.datatypes.raw.RawDataTypeProperties" version="3.9.1">
```

```
          <batchProperties class="com.mirth.connect.plugins.datatypes.raw.RawBatchProperties"
version="3.9.1">
            <splitType>JavaScript</splitType>
            <batchScript></batchScript>
          </batchProperties>
        </inboundProperties>
        <outboundProperties
class="com.mirth.connect.plugins.datatypes.raw.RawDataTypeProperties" version="3.9.1">
          <batchProperties class="com.mirth.connect.plugins.datatypes.raw.RawBatchProperties"
version="3.9.1">
            <splitType>JavaScript</splitType>
            <batchScript></batchScript>
          </batchProperties>
        </outboundProperties>
      </transformer>
      <responseTransformer version="3.9.1">
        <elements/>
        <inboundDataType>RAW</inboundDataType>
        <outboundDataType>RAW</outboundDataType>
        <inboundProperties
class="com.mirth.connect.plugins.datatypes.raw.RawDataTypeProperties" version="3.9.1">
          <batchProperties class="com.mirth.connect.plugins.datatypes.raw.RawBatchProperties"
version="3.9.1">
            <splitType>JavaScript</splitType>
            <batchScript></batchScript>
          </batchProperties>
        </inboundProperties>
        <outboundProperties
class="com.mirth.connect.plugins.datatypes.raw.RawDataTypeProperties" version="3.9.1">
          <batchProperties class="com.mirth.connect.plugins.datatypes.raw.RawBatchProperties"
version="3.9.1">
            <splitType>JavaScript</splitType>
            <batchScript></batchScript>
          </batchProperties>
        </outboundProperties>
      </responseTransformer>
      <filter version="3.9.1">
        <elements/>
      </filter>
      <transportName>Channel Writer</transportName>
      <mode>DESTINATION</mode>
      <enabled>true</enabled>
      <waitForPrevious>true</waitForPrevious>
    </connector>
  </destinationConnectors>
  <preprocessingScript>// Modify the message variable below to pre process data
return message;</preprocessingScript>
  <postprocessingScript>// This script executes once after a message has been processed
// Responses returned from here will be stored as &quot;Postprocessor&quot; in the response
map
return;</postprocessingScript>
  <deployScript>// This script executes once when the channel is deployed
// You only have access to the globalMap and globalChannelMap here to persist data
return;</deployScript>
  <undeployScript>// This script executes once when the channel is undeployed
// You only have access to the globalMap and globalChannelMap here to persist data
return;</undeployScript>
  <properties version="3.9.1">
```

```xml
    <clearGlobalChannelMap>true</clearGlobalChannelMap>
    <messageStorageMode>DEVELOPMENT</messageStorageMode>
    <encryptData>false</encryptData>
    <removeContentOnCompletion>false</removeContentOnCompletion>
    <removeOnlyFilteredOnCompletion>false</removeOnlyFilteredOnCompletion>
    <removeAttachmentsOnCompletion>false</removeAttachmentsOnCompletion>
    <initialState>STARTED</initialState>
    <storeAttachments>true</storeAttachments>
    <metaDataColumns>
      <metaDataColumn>
        <name>SOURCE</name>
        <type>STRING</type>
        <mappingName>mirth_source</mappingName>
      </metaDataColumn>
      <metaDataColumn>
        <name>TYPE</name>
        <type>STRING</type>
        <mappingName>mirth_type</mappingName>
      </metaDataColumn>
    </metaDataColumns>
    <attachmentProperties version="3.9.1">
      <type>None</type>
      <properties/>
    </attachmentProperties>
    <resourceIds class="linked-hash-map">
      <entry>
        <string>Default Resource</string>
        <string>[Default Resource]</string>
      </entry>
    </resourceIds>
  </properties>
  <exportData>
    <metadata>
      <enabled>true</enabled>
      <lastModified>
        <time>1600197048083</time>
        <timezone>America/Los_Angeles</timezone>
      </lastModified>
      <pruningSettings>
        <archiveEnabled>true</archiveEnabled>
      </pruningSettings>
    </metadata>
  </exportData>
</channel>
```

Appendix C – The Enlarged Font

I promised at the start to explain how the screenshots used an enlarged font.

The process is to download Mirth source code and modify one file, then rebuild Mirth. (Actually, the Mirth used for taking the screenshots was run in the Eclipse development environment, so no complete rebuild was performed.) The file is UIConstants.java, in com.mirth.connect.client.ui.

Here is the top part of the file; modified lines end with a // and the original value and are printed in a larger font. Note that I played with the constants only enough to get better-looking screenshots; presumably the way in which the interface of the Administrator is laid out has prevented Mirth and/or NextGen from making font sizes more configurable, so you may run into problems if you build a Mirth using the larger font sizes I used here for demonstration.

```
/*
 * Copyright (c) Mirth Corporation. All rights reserved.
 *
 * http://www.mirthcorp.com
 *
```

```
 * The software in this package is published under the terms of the MPL license a
copy of which has
 * been included with this distribution in the LICENSE.txt file.
 */

package com.mirth.connect.client.ui;

import java.awt.Color;
import java.awt.Font;

import javax.swing.ImageIcon;

import org.apache.commons.lang3.SystemUtils;

/**
 * A constants class for the Mirth UI
 */
public class UIConstants {
    // for EOL stuff
    public static final String EOL_JAVA = "\n";
    public static final String EOL_UNIX = "\n";
    public static final String EOL_WIN32 = "\r\n";
    public static final String EOL_MAC = "\r";
    // for Frame
     public static final int TASK_PANE_WIDTH = 230;//170
    public static final String TITLE_TEXT = "Mirth Connect Administrator";
    public static final int MIRTH_WIDTH = 950;
    public static final int MIRTH_HEIGHT = 650;
    public static final ImageIcon MIRTHCORP_LOGO = new
ImageIcon(com.mirth.connect.client.ui.Frame.class.getResource("images/
mirthcorp_24h.png"));
    public static final ImageIcon MIRTHCONNECT_LOGO_GRAY = new
ImageIcon(com.mirth.connect.client.ui.Frame.class.getResource("images/
mirthconnect_gray_24h.png"));
    public static final String MIRTHCORP_TOOLTIP = "NextGen Healthcare";
    public static final String MIRTHCONNECT_TOOLTIP = "Mirth Connect";
    public static final String MIRTHCORP_URL = "https://www.nextgen.com/products-
and-services/integration-engine";
    public static final String MIRTHCONNECT_URL =
"https://www.nextgen.com/products-and-services/integration-engine";
    public static final String EDIT_FILTER = "Edit Filter";
    public static final String EDIT_TRANSFORMER = "Edit Transformer";
    public static final String EDIT_RESPONSE_TRANSFORMER = "Edit Response";
    public static final String VIEW_NOTIFICATIONS = "Notifications";
    public static final int EDIT_FILTER_TASK_NUMBER = 9;
    public static final int EDIT_TRANSFORMER_TASK_NUMBER = 10;
    public static final int EDIT_RESPONSE_TRANSFORMER_TASK_NUMBER = 11;
    public static final int VIEW_NOTIFICATIONS_TASK_NUMBER = 0;
    // for error checking
    public static final int ERROR_CONSTANT = -1;
    // for JXTables
```

```
    public static final int ROW_HEIGHT = 20;
    public static final int COL_MARGIN = 4;//10
    public static final Color GRID_COLOR = new Color(224, 224, 224);
    public static final int MIN_WIDTH = 125;//75
    public static final int MAX_WIDTH = 300;//200
    public static final int WIDTH_SHORT_MIN = 40;//20
    public static final int WIDTH_SHORT_MAX = 80;//50
    public static final int METADATA_ID_COLUMN_WIDTH = 75;//30
    public static final Color HIGHLIGHTER_COLOR = new Color(240, 240, 240);
    // background colors
    public static final Color BACKGROUND_COLOR = new Color(255, 255, 255);
    public static final Color TITLE_TEXT_COLOR = new Color(0, 0, 0);
    public static final Color HEADER_TITLE_TEXT_COLOR = new Color(255, 255, 255);
    public static final Color COMBO_BOX_BACKGROUND = new Color(220, 220, 220);
    public static final Color JX_CONTAINER_BACKGROUND_COLOR = new Color(0x9EB1C9);
    public static final Color LIGHT_YELLOW = new Color(255, 255, 224);
    // for JSplitPane
    public static final int DIVIDER_SIZE = 12;
    // fonts
    public static final String MONOSPACED_FONT_NAME = SystemUtils.IS_OS_MAC ?
"Courier" : "Monospaced";
    public static final Font TEXTFIELD_PLAIN_FONT = new Font("Tahoma", Font.PLAIN,
16);//11
    public static final Font TEXTFIELD_BOLD_FONT = new Font("Tahoma", Font.BOLD,
16);//11
    public static final Font BANNER_FONT = new Font("Arial", Font.BOLD, 36);
    public static final Font DIALOG_FONT = new Font("Dialog", Font.PLAIN, 18);//12
    public static final Font MONOSPACED_FONT = new Font(MONOSPACED_FONT_NAME,
Font.PLAIN, 18);//12
```

Appendix D – Accessing the Mirth API

More recent versions of Mirth include a REST interface to the server, so that you can send GETs, PUTs and POSTs in order to get back information and/or update the server's settings.

If your server is using Mirth's default "secure" port of 8443, you can direct your browser to https://localhost:8443/api.

You'll then need to log in with the login button in the upper right of the web page, using the same credentials you'd use to log in to the Administrator. Once you are logged in, you can use this web page to send requests to the API and get back responses.

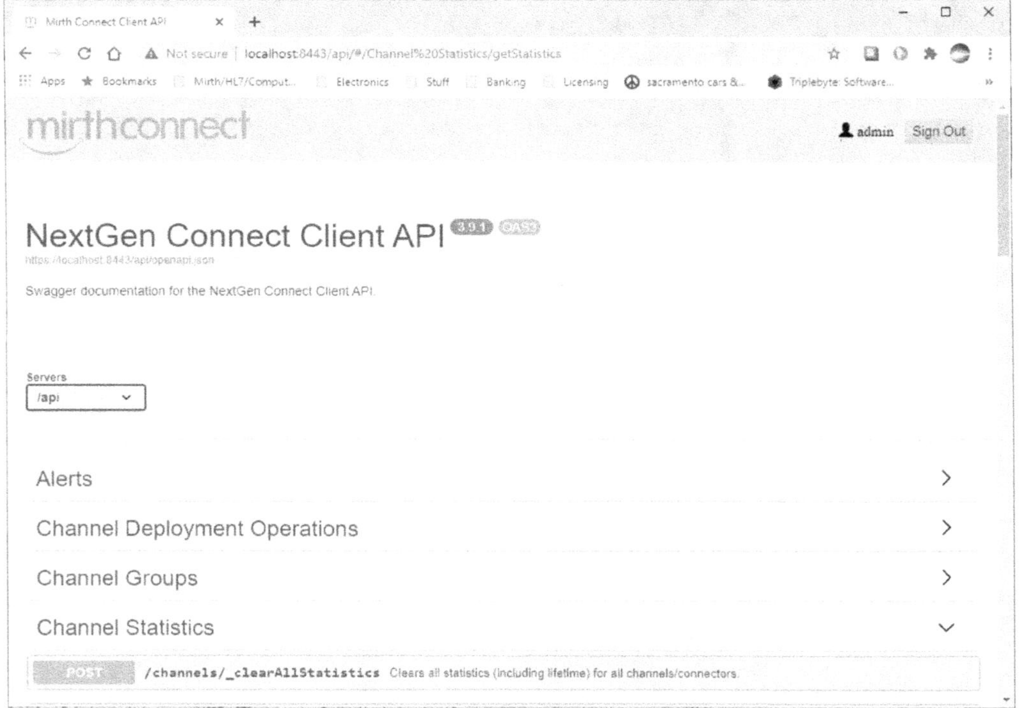

Among other things, this interface is a wonderful way to learn how to interact with various capabilities of the server.

Index

AA....85f., 89f.
Administrator..1ff., 5, 8f., 12, 41, 56, 99, 111f., 114
administrator launcher....2
ADT....59, 85, 93, 96
AE....85
After Processing....36
alerts....3, 79, 81ff.
Amazon S3....38
appdata....57
ar....85f.
Backup Config....41
batch....29ff., 36, 94
channelMap 20ff., 26f., 31, 38f., 73f., 77, 88
channels....1, 3ff., 9, 11f., 14ff., 18f., 33, 45, 47, 50, 73, 79, 86, 91, 99
Code Template libraries....73
configurationMap....39, 99
ConnectorMap....39
cron....35
CSV....15, 18, 25, 28, 30, 36f., 51, 54
CSV format....15
dashboard 3ff., 12f., 17, 22, 27f., 49, 51f., 55f., 65f., 84ff.
data types....9f., 15, 61, 93, 99
database....8, 11, 40ff., 44f., 93f., 97, 99
Delimited Text....15, 24, 33
deploy. 1, 5, 11f., 17, 22, 27, 30f., 48, 50, 52, 55, 65, 77, 82, 90, 97
Destination Mappings....22, 27, 38, 90
DestinationSet....69f.
E4X....29
Edit Transformer....16, 19, 24, 51f., 112
email....5ff., 54, 79f., 82, 85, 99
Errors....84f., 99
EVN....59, 96
Export Results....14
External Script....77
File Reader....33f., 36
File Writer....33, 38, 87, 90
filtering....63, 68
filters....16, 63f., 68, 85
ftp....37f.
generated script....25f., 65, 96
globalChannelMap....39, 77
GlobalMap....39
gmail....6f., 99
HAPI....45ff., 50f., 54, 56, 58ff.
HAPI TestPanel....45, 54, 56, 58ff.
HL7...v, 9ff., 14f., 18, 26, 28, 30f., 45ff., 58ff., 76, 80, 85, 93, 96f., 99
IN1....59
inbound template....27, 93, 95
Java JAR files....77
Java libraries....77
Javascript function....76
JDBC....40
libraries....73, 77
log4j.properties....57
Logger....56, 83
logging....2, 56f.
login window....2
Mapper....20, 25, 28, 30, 51
maps....39
Message Pruning....11
Message Storage....11

message template..24ff., 38, 67f., 70, 91, 96
Message Templates........................24, 68
mirth.properties...................................57
MSH..51, 58ff., 65f., 81, 83, 85, 88ff., 96
Mysql..8
NK1..59
OBR...............................59, 61, 63, 65ff.
OBX..............................53f., 59, 61, 66f.
outbound template...................27, 93, 96
Papercut..6
pgAdmin....................................40f., 44
PID.............11, 52f., 58ff., 66, 76, 96, 99
PID'...52
Postgresql........................8, 40f., 44, 93f.
Process Batch......................................29
PV1...59, 96
raw data..............................9, 11, 13, 79
refresh...12
Reprocess Message.............................55
response messages...............................13
responses...............45, 79, 85f., 89f., 114
Restore Config....................................41
Schedule Type..................................34f.
Send Message.....v, 12, 17, 19, 22, 45, 65
Server Manager.................1f., 42, 44, 56
settings...3, 5ff., 10, 12, 33, 36ff., 41, 114
sftp..37f.
smb..37f.
source filter..67
SourceMap..39
spreadsheet v, 15, 18, 24, 26, 28ff., 50, 93
sql server...8, 94
stack trace...................................82, 84f.
Starting...1, 85
stopping..1
TCP Listener......................................47
transformer..16ff., 23ff., 27f., 30f., 50ff., 59, 63, 66, 70, 73, 76f., 79f., 82ff., 87f., 93, 112
undeploy............................31, 50, 52, 55
Velocity......................................38f., 91
webdav...37f.
webstart.jnlp...2
XML........5, 14, 18ff., 23f., 28ff., 37, 41, 50ff., 58, 83, 88, 93, 97
Z segments...62
$...............................21f., 38f., 82ff., 91

www.ingramcontent.com/pod-product-compliance
Lightning Source LLC
Chambersburg PA
CBHW081516220526
45467CB00010B/2939

* 9 7 9 8 6 8 6 2 8 9 2 6 0 *